I0839725

# Thinking Made Visible
## Movement, Narrative, and the Work of Saul Bass

JACOB A. DICKERSON

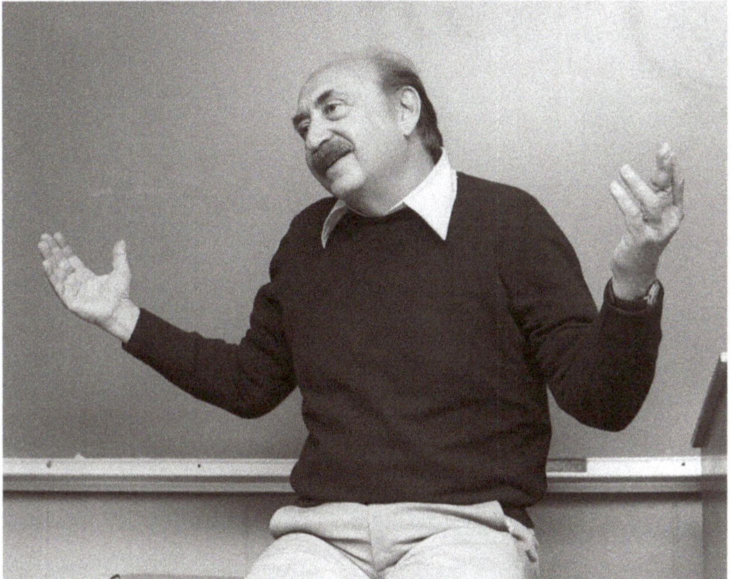

# SAUL

THE MAN WITH THE GOLDEN ARM
'Why Man Creates' a Saul Bass film
United Way

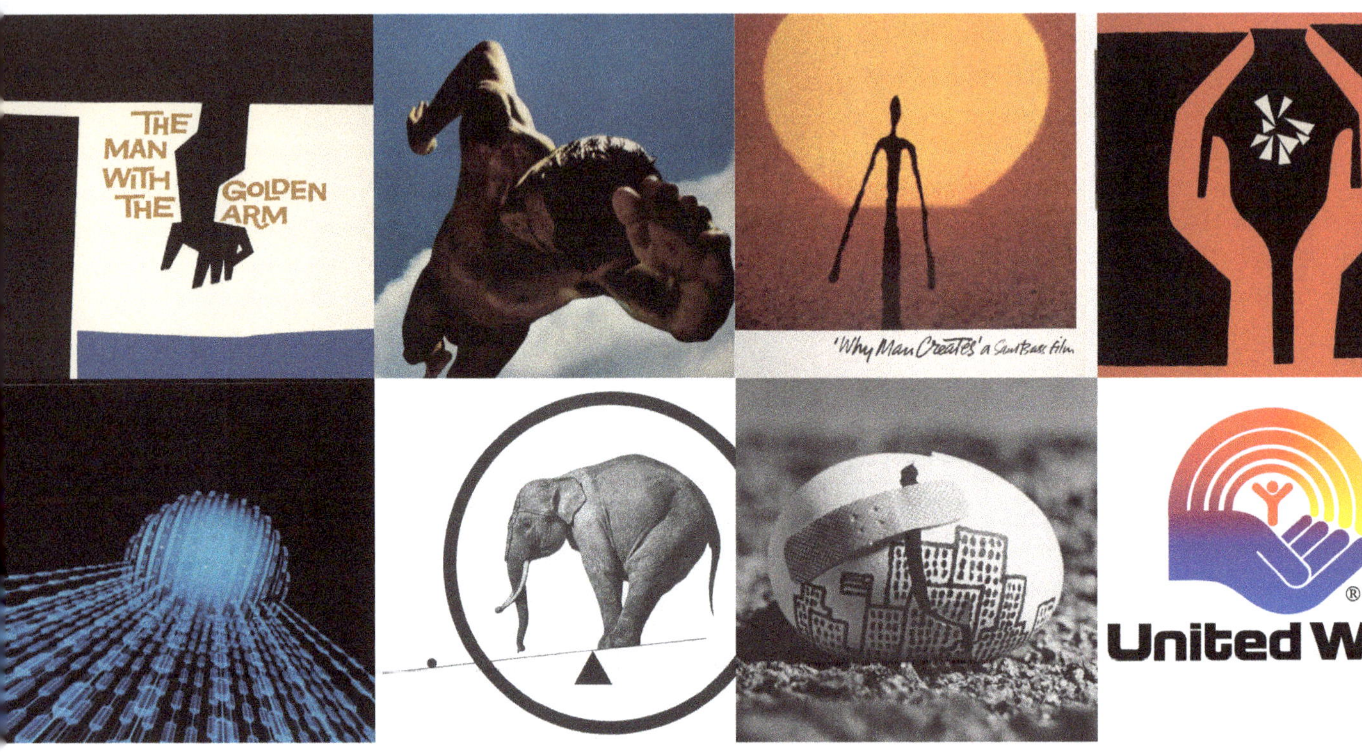

# BASS

**Thinking Made Visible**

## Movement, Narrative, and the Work of Saul Bass

JACOB A. DICKERSON

GRAPHIC DESIGN ARCHIVES
CHAPBOOK SERIES: SEVEN

RIT PRESS

2025

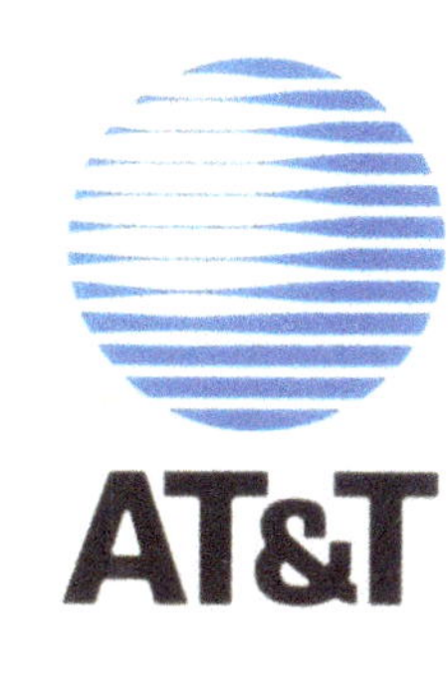



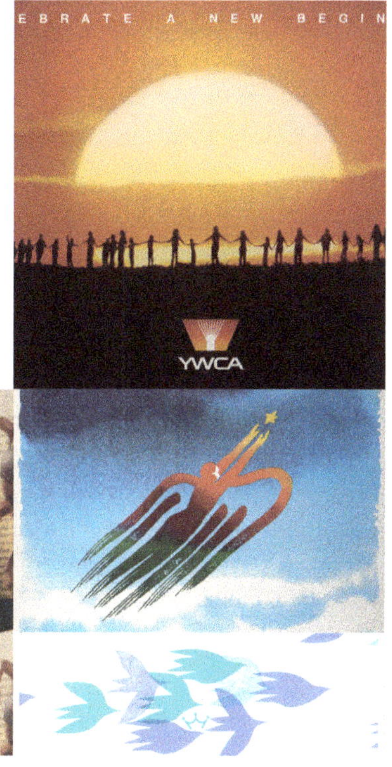



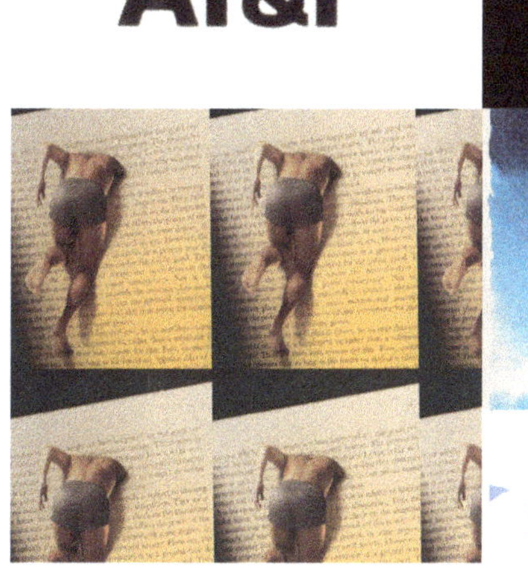

# Thinking Made Visible
## Movement, Narrative, and the Work of Saul Bass

JACOB A. DICKERSON

GRAPHIC DESIGN ARCHIVES
CHAPBOOK SERIES: SEVEN

RIT PRESS
90 Lomb Memorial Drive
Rochester, New York 14623-5604

We gather on the traditional territory of the Onöndowa'ga:' or "the people of the Great Hill." In English, they are known as Seneca people, "the keeper of the western door." They are one of the six nations that make up the sovereign Haudenosaunee Confederacy.

We honor the land on which RIT was built and recognize the unique relationship that the Indigenous stewards have with this land. That relationship is the core of their traditions, cultures, and histories.

We recognize the history of genocide, colonization, and assimilation of Indigenous people that took place on this land. Mindful of these histories, we work towards understanding, acknowledging, and ultimately reconciliation.


Copyright © 2025 Rochester Institute of Technology and Jacob A. Dickerson

No part of this book may be reproduced in any form or by any mechanical or electronic means without permission of the publisher and/or the copyright holders, except in the case of brief quotations.

Published and distributed by:
RIT Press
90 Lomb Memorial Drive
Rochester, New York 14623
https://press.rit.edu

ISBN 978-1-956313-12-3 (print)
ISBN 978-1-956313-13-0 (electronic)
Printed in the USA

**Library of Congress Cataloging-in-Publication Data**

| | |
|---|---|
| Names: | Dickerson, Jacob, 1980– author. |
| Title: | Thinking made visible : movement, narrative, and the work of Saul Bass / Jacob Dickerson. |
| Description: | Rochester, New York : RIT Press, [2024] | Includes bibliographical references. |
| Identifiers: | LCCN 2024027443 (print) | LCCN 2024027444 (ebook) | ISBN 9781956313123 (paperback) | ISBN 9781956313130 (pdf) |
| Subjects: LCSH: | Bass, Saul—Criticism and interpretation. |
| Classification: | LCC NC999.4.B38 D53 2024 (print) | LCC NC999.4.B38 (ebook) | DDC 741.6/74092—dc23/eng/20240722 |

LC record available at https://lccn.loc.gov/2024027443
LC ebook record available at https://lccn.loc.gov/2024027444

Black and white photos of Saul Bass, May 1979; RITArc. 0784, RIT University Image collection; RIT Archives, Rochester Institute of Technology.

# Movement, Narrative, and the Work of Saul Bass

JACOB A. DICKERSON

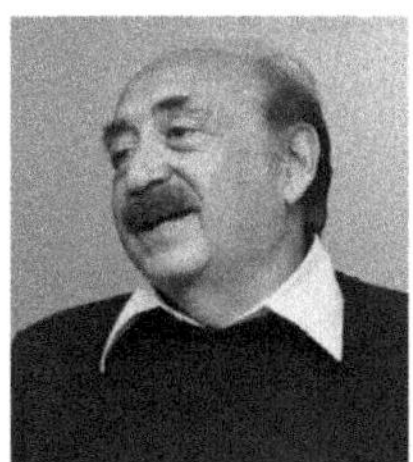

## Introduction

In an unpublished manuscript later described in his biography, Saul Bass wrote that trademarks for corporate identity are, "in a certain sense, thinking made visible."[1] This idea was part of his larger design philosophy; he had also described design with the same phrase. Bass's philosophy was not entirely unique, since the phrase "thought made visible" is a relatively common descriptor of modern or conceptual art.[2] However, Bass's use of the word "thinking" rather than "thought" is revealing because it suggests the presentation of an ongoing process of conceptualization rather than a fully formed idea. In other words, a logo, or a poster, or a movie title sequence represents not some embodiment of the designer's understanding, but an invitation for the viewer to explore meaning along with the designer and share in the experience of the artwork, the brand, the film, or even a physical space.

1 Bass and Kirkham, 281.

2 See, for instance, Mel Bochner's 1995 exhibition at Yale University titled "Thought Made Visible" (Field et al., 1995), or an academic discussion of contemporary dance that utilizes the phrase in its title (Stevens and McKechnie, 2005).

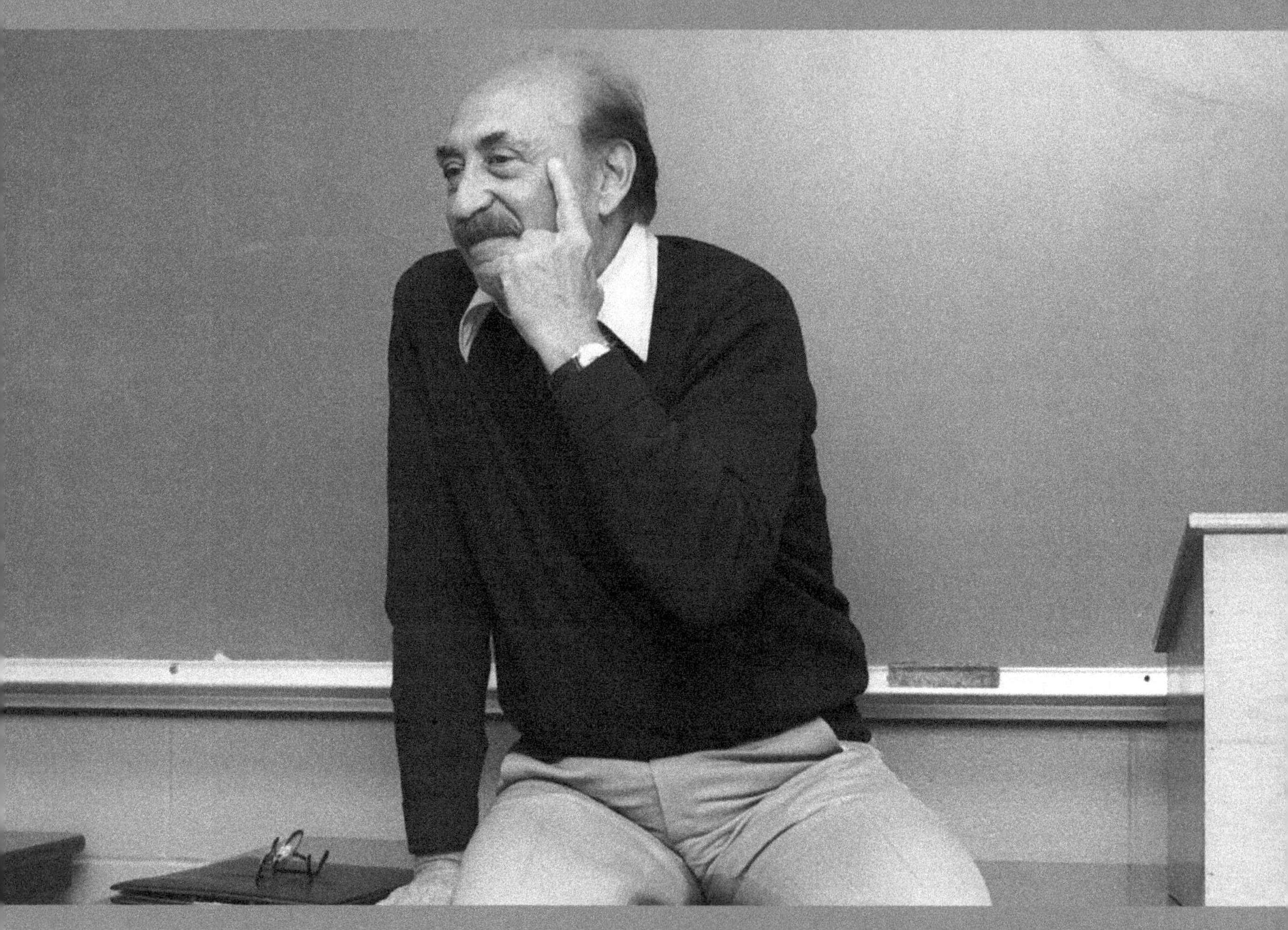

3   Horak, Saul Bass: Anatomy of Film Design, 63.

4   In this book, references to Bass's work
    primarily include his logos, posters, or
    architectural designs unless otherwise specified.
    Movement is much more obvious in a film or
    animation sequence.

5   Horak, 129.

Bass's work spanned nearly sixty years in fields ranging from corporate identity to the film industry to architecture. He utilized nearly all possible media, including print, film, animation, and even retail buildings. In addition to his design work, Bass was a filmmaker, having directed a feature film (*Phase IV*, 1974) and a number of short documentaries, including the 1968 Oscar-winning *Why Man Creates* (funded by Kaiser Aluminum). Like that film, these were funded primarily by corporate sponsors. While on the surface it may appear as if Bass's work is incredibly varied, there are nonetheless a number of threads tying most of it together. There are some clear and consistent elements in the "Bass Brand,"[3] the most striking of which is the sense of movement—even within the posters and corporate logos. It is this movement that gets to the heart of what makes his designs so effective. To read the image, the viewer is asked to mentally move through time or to imagine what comes next. In this way, Bass's designs create an experience for the viewer, one that is rooted in a narrative conceptualization of the image itself.[4] Indeed, as Jan-Christopher Horak, a former director of the UCLA Film & Television Archive and the author of *Saul Bass: Anatomy of Film Design*, notes, Bass's film posters "often reduced a film's narrative content to a single iconic image."[5]

Perhaps the best example of this is Bass's iconic poster for film producer and director Otto Preminger's *The Man with the Golden Arm* (1955), which features a disembodied arm reaching down from the top of the image. The hand's bent fingers suggest that they are about to grab something or, perhaps, are flexing in pain, anger, or frustration. The film's title sequence, also designed by Bass, is animated with

6  "Review: *The Man with The Golden Arm*," *Variety*, December 31, 1955.

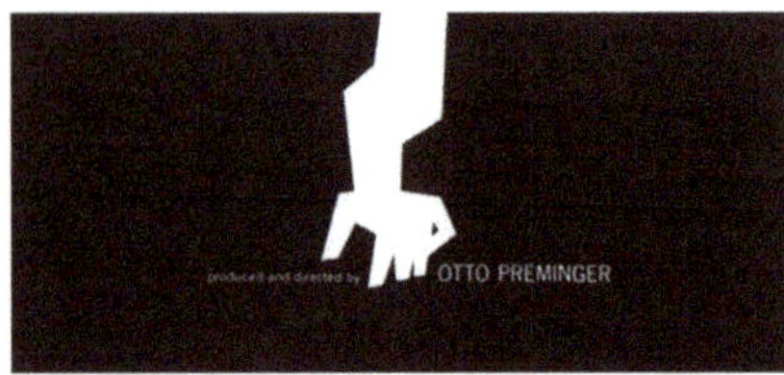

**Figure 1.**

Final image of Bass's title sequence for *The Man with the Golden Arm* (1955).

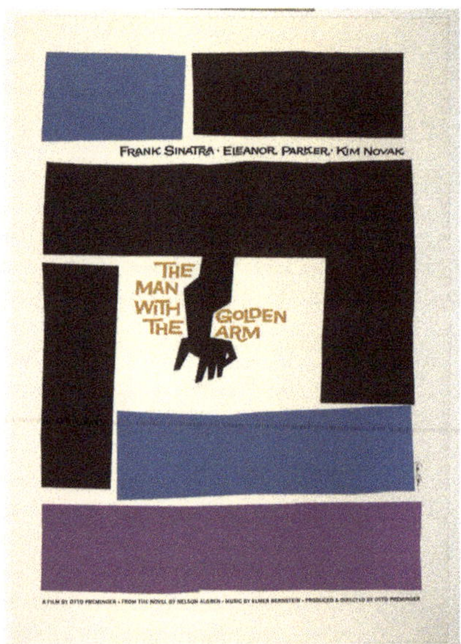


**Figure 2.**

Poster for *The Man with the Golden Arm* (1955). Saul Bass Collection, Cary Graphic Arts Collection at the Wallace Library, Rochester Institute of Technology.

white bars sliding into the frame at various angles, at times resembling horizontal window blinds or vertical prison bars all tilting askew. It concludes with four intersecting vertical lines morphing into the shape of the arm. When examined as a still frame (see Figure 1), the hand appears to be descending, grabbing Preminger's director credit. The distortion of the arm evokes a sense of movement, while the placement of the fingers gives the impression that the hand may pluck the credit from the screen. The effect is amplified when the arm is placed on the original poster for the film (see Figure 2). The hand is still moving down to grab Preminger's credit, but it is also forcing its way through the title, clearing a path. True to the film's addiction theme and *Variety's* description of Frank Sinatra's character as a "drug slave," the arm cannot be stopped or controlled, but instead manipulates the image for its own accommodation.[6]

Bass's work was an essential piece of the American visual landscape in the second half of the twentieth century, imbuing logos with motion and film titles with stories. With that in mind, this chapbook explores Bass's sense of movement and its connection to narrative and experience. Since his film title sequences have been examined in great detail elsewhere (e.g., Horak's book), this analysis focuses primarily upon his poster and logo designs as well as a major architectural project that has been given little attention, but which provides insight into most of Bass's work: his 1981 redesign of the Exxon/Esso service stations, which marked the beginning of the gas-station environment as we know it today. Focusing primarily on his corporate work requires some exploration of the Bauhaus design concepts that influenced Bass, as well as theories of narrative thought in which brain functions

7   Hope Preminger, speaking at the Saul Bass
    Celebration in New York City, May 23, 1996.
    Saul Bass Collection, Cary Graphic Arts
    Collection at the Wallace Library, Rochester
    Institute of Technology.

8   Martin Scorsese, foreword to Saul Bass:
    *A Life in Film and Design*, by Jennifer Bass and
    Pat Kirkham, vi–vii.

are connected to everyday experience. From this latter perspective, narratives are conceptualized as forming the basis of conscious experience, and it is with this idea that the power of Bass's work becomes evident. It lies in his ability to think narratively and portray that thought in a single, experience-encompassing image. As Hope Preminger, wife of Otto Preminger—with whom Bass worked on a number of films—said during his memorial, "The genius of Saul Bass was that he was able to make one single image convey what a film was all about."[7]

Before diving into an analysis of Bass's work, however, this book first gives a brief overview of Bass's story. While biography is not a central purpose here, it is nonetheless essential to an understanding of Bass and his work. That work, because of its familiarity and centrality to American visual culture, can always be talked about in the present tense. His logo for Girl Scouts of America is instantly recognizable and conjures up images of cookie sales and memories of campfires. As Martin Scorsese has written, Bass's work addresses everyone. His designs are timeless; however, they are also grounded in our past, offering a vision of "a shared sense of the world" as it existed at the moment of their creation.[8] In a career that began in the 1930s and spanned six decades, Saul Bass captured innumerable shared moments.

**Becoming Saul Bass**

One of the most important aspects of understanding Bass as a designer is to understand how he viewed his own place in the world. By all accounts, Bass was a humble man who wanted primarily to do good work that mattered to the world and to others. In his tribute during a memorial at the

9  Herb Yager and Richard Farson, speaking at the Saul Bass Memorial at the Academy of Motion Picture Arts and Sciences in Los Angeles, 1996. Saul Bass Collection, Cary Graphic Arts Collection at the Wallace Library, Rochester Institute of Technology.

10  Horak, 4.

11  Herb Yager, speaking at the Saul Bass Celebration in New York City, May 23, 1996. Saul Bass Collection, Cary Graphic Arts Collection at the Wallace Library, Rochester Institute of Technology.

12  Carl Bell and Elmer Bernstein, speaking at the Saul Bass Memorial at the Academy of Motion Picture Arts and Sciences in Los Angeles, 1996. Saul Bass Collection, Cary Graphic Arts Collection at the Wallace Library, Rochester Institute of Technology.

13  Bass and Kirkham.

14  Horak, 35.

Academy of Motion Picture Arts and Sciences, Bass's longtime business partner, Herb Yager, told a story of a conversation in which Bass talked about how he had hoped his life would unfold. He reportedly said, "I always wanted to be Saul Bass." At the same event, Richard Farson, the president of the International Design Conference in Aspen (IDCA), said Bass once told him that he didn't want people to look at his work and say, "That's Saul Bass." Instead, he hoped they would say, "That's somebody."[9] These views reflect Bass's intentional construction of a personal brand. While Horak describes the "Bass brand" in terms of commonalities within his designs,[10] Bass the man also had a very distinct brand. This personality brand was very much rooted in his past and in his own insecurities, which were mentioned repeatedly by those honoring him at various memorials. Together, Bass's past and his insecurities created his sense of humility. As Yager said, "He never saw himself as an artist with a capital A. He was just a guy doing a job and it was a job he liked and that he was good at."[11] There was no extricating Bass from his designs. Animator Carl Bell described Bass as "the man, the artist, the work all at once and at the same time." And, as Elmer Bernstein noted, Bass used his art to "[make] the world a lighter place. But the light came from inside of Saul."[12]

Saul Bass was born in the Bronx to Jewish immigrants on May 8, 1920. At home, his family spoke only Yiddish; he did not learn English until he entered school. He described his neighborhood as being on the other side of the proverbial tracks, though the family did better financially than others.[13] He graduated from high school at fifteen, already being recognized for his artistic work.[14] He had been the arts editor for his school's literary publication and had received two

15  Bass and Kirkham.

16  Bass and Kirkham, 3.

**Figure 3.**

Keio Department Store Wrapping Paper
(1964).

awards from the School Art League of New York City.
Due to the financial situation during the Great Depression,
Bass was unable to attend college. Instead, he worked while
attending night classes at the Art Students League. After
working two jobs only loosely related to art, he began
to search for work at an advertising agency, landing at
a small studio—making $20 a week—that created trade
advertisements for United Artists. By 1941, he had moved up
to a salary of $100 per week and was working for Twentieth
Century Fox.[15]

Bass had developed an early interest in art, which he
attributed to his father, who had given him a box of crayons
with which he made his first memory of creating art. Aaron
Bass, Saul's father and a furrier, had a penchant for drawing
flowers and birds and was skilled in creating decorative paper
cut-outs. As Bass described them, his father's paper creations
were "a whole world."[16] Perhaps it was his father's art that
inspired Bass's paper cut-out style designs for posters for
movies such as *Anatomy of a Murder* (1959), *Saint Joan* (1957),
and *Nine Hours to Rama* (1963); or perhaps it was Aaron's
birds that inspired Saul's design in 1964 for Keio department
store's wrapping paper (see Figure 3). The paper, featuring
stylized blue doves on a white background, is indicative of
Bass's habit of designing even still images that appear to be
in motion. The doves' slightly elongated bodies and wings
give the impression of birds in flight, moving across the paper.
This concept of motion is rooted in the Bauhaus school of art
that so inspired Bass.

17  Bass and Kirkham; Horak.

18  Bass and Kirkham, 9.

19  Gyorgy Kepes, Language of Vision
    (Chicago: Paul Theobald, 1944), 44.

20  Kepes, Language of Vision, 24.

21  Bass and Kirkham.

Bass discovered Gyorgy Kepes's *Language of Vision* (1944) and Laszlo Moholy-Nagy's *Vision in Motion* (1947) shortly after leaving Twentieth Century Fox and starting work for half the salary at Blaine Thompson Company, a New York advertising firm. Bass had disliked working in movie publicity because he did not have the freedom to design posters in the way he wanted, so upon the move, he declared that he would never work in film advertising again.[17]

It was also during this time that Bass began to study with Gyorgy Kepes at Brooklyn College. Not only was Bass moved by the Bauhaus design concepts—he once said that Kepes "set me on fire. . . . I felt . . . like my pores were palpitating"—but he was also drawn to the psychological dimensions of Kepes's work.[18] In a description of what he calls "the psychological field," Kepes claims that an "image is an organism that reaches out to the dimensions of understanding beyond the sensory radius."[19] He is concerned with the spatial forces within an image, claiming that power can be found in the space between objects, allowing for spatial forces to act upon them. In other words, space allows for movement and action.[20] As a result of his work with Kepes, Bass's own work was simplified and became more abstract. Backgrounds became sparse and there was greater emphasis on geometric shapes. Shortly thereafter, he won his first award from the New York Art Directors Club for an advertisement for a hair product, the concept of which had come from one of Kepes's exercises on spatial tension (see Figure 4).[21]

The image shows an elephant inside of a circle, balancing carefully on a seesaw with a ball at the opposite end while the ad copy celebrates "absolute control and perfect balance."

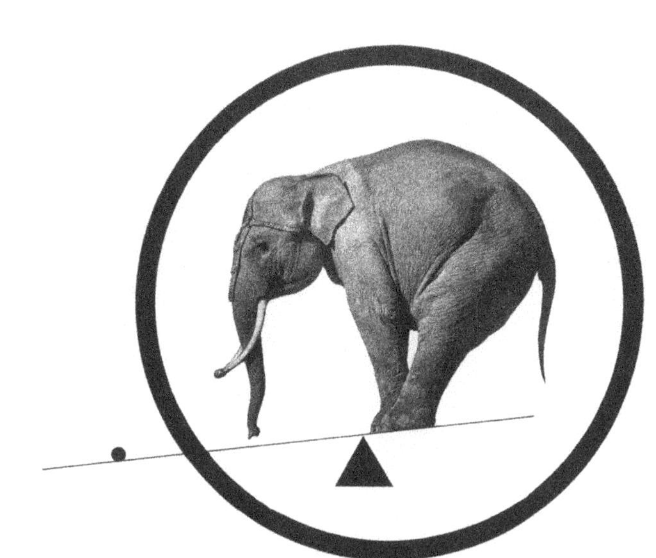


**Figure 4.**

Tylon Cold Wave advertisement (1945).

22  Horak, 55.

23  Kepes, 24.

Kepes's claim is that objects in an image generate "different experiences of space," depending on their placement. And, importantly, more objects lead to a greater "sensation of space" and suggest movement and direction. In Bauhaus design, geometric shapes help create an illusion of movement based on their placement within the image. They also help to guide the eye as it moves around the different elements within the design.[22] The objects "force the eye to orient and explore" the entire image.[23] Bass's advertisement for Tylon contains at least five objects: the ball, the seesaw, the fulcrum, the elephant, and the circle. The spatial relationship between them guides the viewer's eye and understanding. The eye is naturally drawn to the large circle, forcing the viewer to consider the elephant's precarious position. The curve of the circle, along with the seesaw, then directs the viewer to the ball, at which point they may consider the fulcrum and the physics that might make such a pose possible. Since the mind expects that the elephant would weigh more than the ball and, therefore, fling it into the air, the viewer can also begin to imagine the elephant leaning backward slightly, causing the ball to rise on the other end of the seesaw. It is in the spatial relationships of the objects that the image's effectiveness is found. One can be certain of the control necessary for the elephant (and the ball) to remain motionless, attaching that to the product. But what is most important here is the simplicity of the image's structure. The viewer's eye and thought process are controlled by the careful placement of only a few objects. And it is in their spatial relationships that movement is suggested.

In Bauhaus design, representing objects in motion is a central way that the design itself contributes to the creation of a shared experience. The narrative put forth in the image is constructed

24 Laszlo Moholy-Nagy, *Vision in Motion* (Chicago: Paul Theobald, 1947), 12.

25 Pamela Haskin, "Saul, Can You Make Me a Title? Interview with Saul Bass," *Film Quarterly* 50, no. 1 (Autumn 1996): 13.

26 Martin Scorsese, speaking at the Saul Bass Celebration in New York City, May 23, 1996. Saul Bass Collection, Cary Graphic Arts Collection at the Wallace Library, Rochester Institute of Technology.

27 Julian Binod, speaking at the Saul Bass Celebration in New York City, May 23, 1996. Saul Bass Collection, Cary Graphic Arts Collection at the Wallace Library, Rochester Institute of Technology.

28 Haskin, 35.

by both the artist, who arranges the elements, and the viewer, who must navigate the visual space and reassemble that narrative. In this way, the artist and the viewer work together. That shared experience is key to establishing emotion within the viewer. From a Bauhaus perspective, representing moving objects in a static image is to put vision in motion, or to capture the simultaneity of space and time. Through vision in motion, the artist "recreates mentally and emotionally the original motion."[24] In his own description of his film titles, Bass claimed that he "saw the title as a way of conditioning the audience, so that when the film actually began, viewers would already have an emotional resonance with it."[25] As Scorsese described Bass's work, a film's poster "was the dream . . . of what you were going to see," while his titles "pierce deeply into the soul of the films they were introducing."[26]

Bass integrated the animated titles with film publicity very early in his work, creating a sense of branding for the film. Binod's description of Bass's art provides a useful distillation of what he was able to achieve through his film publicity and titles. He says that there are two "arms" in Bass's work: one that distills meaning to a single image and one in which meaning only becomes obvious in sequence with other images.[27] For instance, the arm in the titles and posters for *The Man with the Golden Arm* came to represent the film so strongly that when it opened in New York, its only representation on the marquee was Bass's distorted arm—without the title.[28] Bass's knack for making still images appear to be in motion also has roots in the film. Following an argument with director Preminger in planning for the film's titles, Bass began to think about the possibility of

29 Haskin, 14.

30 Horak, 55–56.

31 Haskin, 16.

32 Moholy-Nagy, 25.

33 Moholy-Nagy, 27.

static images in the sequence, saying "there might be a sort of kinetic effect with a series of staccato images."[29] For Bass, movement was central to conveying meaning in his art.

**Bauhaus and Movement**

As examined earlier, in Bauhaus design geometric shapes create an illusion of movement and guide the eye as it explores the image in search of meaning. This sense of movement creates a relationship between the work and the viewer "until the experience reaches full integration."[30] For Bass, that integration allowed the audience to see from a new perspective ordinary experiences and things they already knew. He says that one of his driving ideas "was to transform the ordinary into the extraordinary."[31]

The Bauhaus aesthetic views art as something to be experienced and, through that experience, something that provides for a richer, more complete social and cultural life. Moholy-Nagy suggests that art can contribute to the enrichment of a society that has replaced experience with information and entertainment. He claims that a new generation of artists can help society understand experience as a key to seeing "the essential purpose of living."[32] He goes on to make an explicit connection to experience, saying imagery "is inherent in and connected with the sensory experiences which express a concept beyond the intellectual grasp."[33] For Moholy-Nagy, art balances emotional and intellectual existence. Here is the basis for Bass's understanding of art's function. Bass embraced the notion that human beings are the sum of their experiences, and art provides an emotional connection between people. According to artist Gyorgy Kepes, art does not simply connect the mind to experience; it is

34  Kepes, 15.

35  Moholy-Nagy, 42.

36  Kepes, 29.

37  Ivan Chermayeff, speaking at the Saul Bass
    Celebration in New York City, May 23, 1996.
    Saul Bass Collection, Cary Graphic Arts
    Collection at the Wallace Library, Rochester
    Institute of Technology.

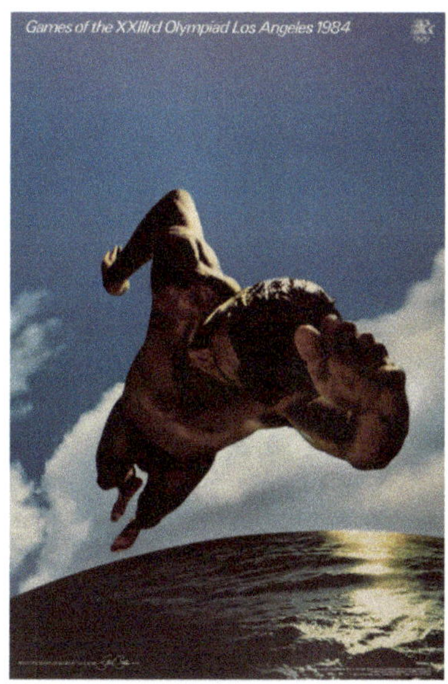


**Figure 5.**

Summer Olympics Poster (1984). Saul Bass
Collection, Cary Graphic Arts Collection,
at the Wallace Library, Rochester Institute
of Technology.

experience. As he says, "To perceive an image is to participate in a forming process . . . Independent of what one 'sees,' every experiencing of a visual image is a forming . . . a 'plastic' experience."34

From this perspective, the effect of art emerges from the relationships among elements of a design. As Moholy-Nagy argues, if elements of a work of art are to be coherent, "they must become the construction elements of complex relationships."35 As a result, an emphasis on abstract design elements being placed within what Kepes calls "fields of spatial forces" became a hallmark of Bauhaus design.36 It would also become central to the look of Bass's work. As graphic designer Ivan Chermayeff stated at Bass's New York memorial, Bass "saw things very three dimensionally. Moving, animated, and alive."37 The idea of being alive would be central to much of Bass's design work for various humanitarian and environmental causes, as will be examined later in this book. But three-dimensional movement is a prominent aspect in all of his work. It can be seen most explicitly in work similar to his poster for the 1984 Los Angeles Olympics (see Figure 5). In this poster, a swimmer moves toward the viewer, seeming to come directly out of the image. The swimmer's arms are at dynamic angles—the rear arm is flexed, demonstrating strength, and the front arm is extended toward the viewer, seeming to emerge directly from the image. The poster achieves this effect using extension distortion, a photographic technique that plays with perspective in such a way as to extend distance, making the swimmer seem longer than he might otherwise appear, an effect amplified by his spatial relationship to the poster's background. Interestingly, the difference in perspective

38  This image was not able to be reproduced for
    this book. However, it can be viewed online at
    https://filmartgallery.com/products/sba-nine-
    hours-to-rama.

between the swimmer and the background creates a distortion effect similar to parallax or the 2.5D animation currently employed by designers to give still photographs a sense of movement by separating and independently distorting the background and foreground objects. Although Bass's poster and the modern technique are not necessarily related in a technical sense, the poster nonetheless employs a similar theory in order to create a sense of movement.

A water-covered Earth stands in the background, giving the illusion that the swimmer is moving over the surface of the world. In this way, there is not merely three-dimensional movement for the viewer, but also a conceptual dimensionality for the swimmer himself. He is not moving up or forward, but around and beyond. He is Superman flying around the planet while simultaneously coming toward the viewer, perhaps representing the powerful athletes moving toward the United States.

The Olympic athletes may be moving toward hopeful glory, but Bass's unused poster design for the 1963 British film *Nine Hours to Rama* uses a remarkably similar three-dimensional perspective. The film provides a fictionalized account of Nathuram Godse in the nine hours prior to his assassination of Mohandas Gandhi in 1948. Bass's poster depicts a fallen Gandhi clutching a flower in his outstretched left hand.[38] Gandhi is represented as unable to continue moving toward his ultimate goal of peace, though he is depicted as still striving, even in death. The image is in a paper cut-out style reminiscent of Bass's work on *Anatomy of a Murder* (1959) and, later, on *Such Good Friends* (1971). Like the swimmer's, the rear arm is flexed, providing the power for Ghandi to push himself forward while the front arm reaches toward the viewer. Ghandi's body is not elongated but is nonexistent, reflecting the loss of his life while his ideals live and move on. Another difference in the three-dimensional mode of the film poster is that the hand does not appear to reach toward the viewer, but the flower clasped in Ghandi's hand extends beyond the image, giving the viewer the impression that Ghandi himself continued beyond the boundaries of his life. Indeed, as is demonstrated in the analyses throughout this book, playing with boundaries and grasping hands are central tenets of much of Bass's work, with boundaries being broken and hands used as tools to reach, aspire, and protect—particularly in his work related to the socially caring and responsible ideals also relevant to Ghandi. Although the Olympic and *Rama* posters are thematically and stylistically quite different, the parallelism of the bodies' positioning is clear. In that way, they both provide a glimpse into Bass's three-dimensional thought.

Bass presents an interesting reversal of the image of the swimmer in his cover for the UCLA Extension catalog in 1987 (see Figure 6, showing the design in poster form). In this image, a man appears to be diving into a book. Here, he is moving away from the viewer, but he is nonetheless swimming in and through the words. Bass's use of the third dimension clearly establishes a perception of forward movement. The man is moving forward, but his direction away from the viewer invites the viewer to move with him. He is moving away from, but in the same direction as, the viewer. In the first poster, the third dimension suggests that the athletes are coming to the viewer, but in the second the viewer is asked to come along and dive into the poster's world.

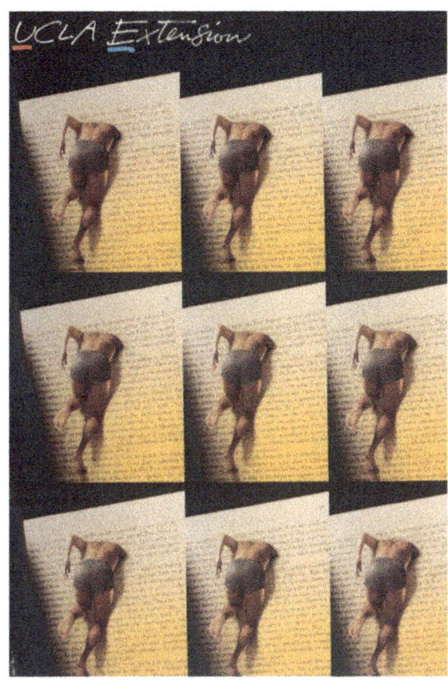


**Figure 6.**

UCLA Extension Poster (1987). Saul Bass Collection, Cary Graphic Arts Collection at the Wallace Library, Rochester Institute of Technology. Courtesy UCLA Extension.

39  Marilyn Laurie, speaking at the Saul Bass
    Celebration in New York City, May 23, 1996.
    Saul Bass Collection, Cary Graphic Arts
    Collection at the Wallace Library, Rochester
    Institute of Technology.

40  Bass and Kirkham, 330.

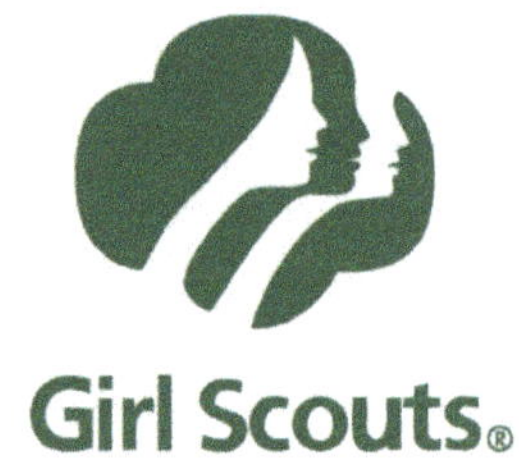

**Figure 7.**

Girl Scouts of the USA logo (1978).
Image courtesy of Girl Scouts of the USA.

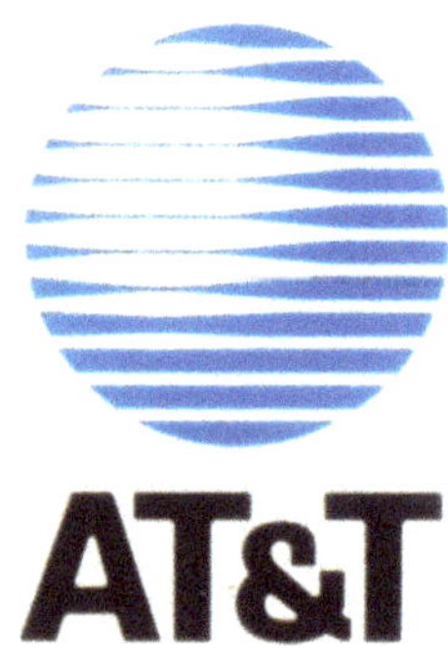

**Figure 8.**
AT&T Logo (1984). Courtesy
of AT&T Archives and History Center.

The UCLA Extension is a continuing-education institution offering open-enrollment courses for nontraditional students. Bass's cover design invites the viewer to literally move into a world that will provide the better life promised by furthering one's education.

This concept of motion is central to many of Bass's designs and is also present in his two-dimensional work. It can be seen, for instance, in his logo for the Girl Scouts of the USA (see Figure 7). The logo, an updated version of which is still in use, shows three girls perhaps standing shoulder-to-shoulder, but it also suggests the forward movement of a single girl. In this way, the logo represents unity and solidarity, but also individuality. The forward movement of the single girl also represents her maturation, moving forward through time from childhood to adolescence.

A more subtle sense of movement is present in Bass's logo for AT&T (see Figure 8). Bass had been the architect of one of the largest branding projects in history with his logo and identity designs for Bell Systems in 1969. When the company began the divestiture process after a Justice Department ruling in 1983, it seemed natural that Bass would be involved. It is telling that Marilyn Laurie, head of public relations for AT&T from 1987 to 1998, spoke at the Saul Bass Celebration after his death. She described him as "part of the fabric of AT&T."[39] In the more recent logo, Bass was able to suggest both movement and a third dimension by widening the white lines. The change gives the impression of a turning sphere, with a light shining in the upper left quadrant of the logo. Indeed, Bass described the logo as representing "the world girded by information."[40] AT&T would later literalize the suggestions

41  An example of this as a tag to the 1984
    AT&T commercial is available at
    https://www.youtube.com/watch?v=ffNIpwbbDqQ

42  Marilyn Laurie, speaking at the Saul Bass
    Celebration in New York City, May 23, 1996.
    Saul Bass Collection, Cary Graphic Arts
    Collection at the Wallace Library, Rochester
    Institute of Technology. The stripes were
    originally added to the vans during the 1969
    rebranding process and then modified for the 1984
    divestiture redesign.

43  Bass and Kirkham, 330.

of movement and a third dimension in their 2005 and 2016 redesigns of the logo, adding curves to more clearly give depth to the image.

Bass himself made the three-dimensionality and motion of the logo explicit in TV spots for the newly reorganized company. In the ads, strings of prisms move toward and around a spinning sphere, which then morphs into the two-dimensional logo.[41] The image from the commercial was reproduced in poster form (see Figure 9). The prisms provide a sense of not only movement and depth, but also speed. For AT&T, information not only girded the world—it moved at the speed of light. AT&T held the concept of speed at the center of its newly emerging corporate identity. Laurie described the white lines in the logo and the stripes added to the company's repair vehicles as "racing stripes."[42] Bass's conceptualization of information circling the world at great speeds turned out to be prescient of the way we would come to think of telecommunication. He would reflect on this in a later interview with Joe Morgenstern, saying, "Little did I know . . . that the 'Information Superhighway' would become the buzzword of the 1990s."[43]

And there is evidence on the "information superhighway" of Bass's enduring influence on graphic design, particularly some of his more famous logos, including AT&T's. An important recent trend in design—particularly, though not exclusively, in the presentation of iconography in mobile interfaces—is flat design. And in the case of logos or icons, images tend to include a single-color background with a symbol or a contrasting color. Very clearly informed by the Bauhaus style, flat design presents a two-dimensional image

**Figure 9.**

AT&T Poster (1984).
Saul Bass Collection, Cary Graphic
Arts Collection at the Wallace Library,
Rochester Institute of Technology.
Courtesy of AT&T Archives and
History Center.

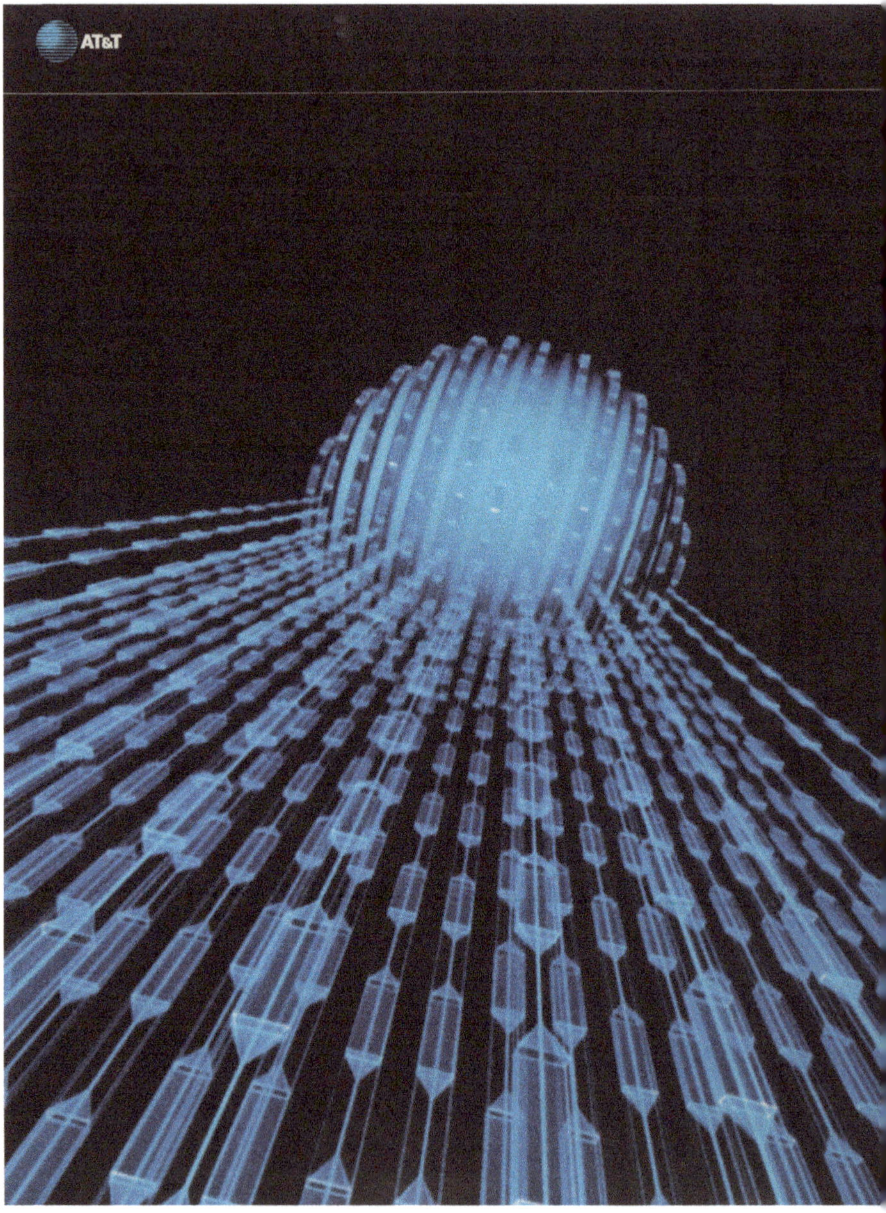

and is entirely utilitarian. It is intended to provide relatively invisible guidance through the user experience. Flat design is most clearly seen in Microsoft's tile interface, in navigational images for things such as shopping carts on websites, or in the icons for apps on your smartphone. Many of Bass's logos would seem to be custom-made for the flat style, especially a logo such as the one he designed for Warner Communications in 1974, which featured an abstract "W" over a rounded blue field. Flat design emerged as a response to the use of realistic images in design, which, in comparison, created clutter in the user experience by incorporating an excess of detail—the very thing the Bauhaus movement taught Bass to avoid.

**Abstraction**

Following his exposure to Bauhaus artists such as Moholy-Nagy and Kepes, Bass stated that his own work became more dynamic and abstract.[44] Bass recognized that reducing sensory perception more effectively engages the viewer and that the more generalized an image is, the better it may interact with the viewer's memory, connecting to multiple objects and experiences in their lives.[45]

This is evident in Bass's use of abstract, reductive images in much of his logo design. Bass's logos often serve more to embody an organization's ethos rather than to provide a representation of their products or services. For instance, in his design for what is now the Boys and Girls Clubs of America—a logo adopted in 1980 and still in use—Bass presents an image of two hands clasped. That interpretation, however, only becomes obvious when viewed in relationship to the organization's name or, as shown here on a poster, with photographs of hands (see Figure 10). Of the symbol,

Figure 10.

Boys Clubs of America Poster (1980).
Saul Bass Collection, Cary Graphic
Arts Collection at the Wallace Library,
Rochester Institute of Technology.


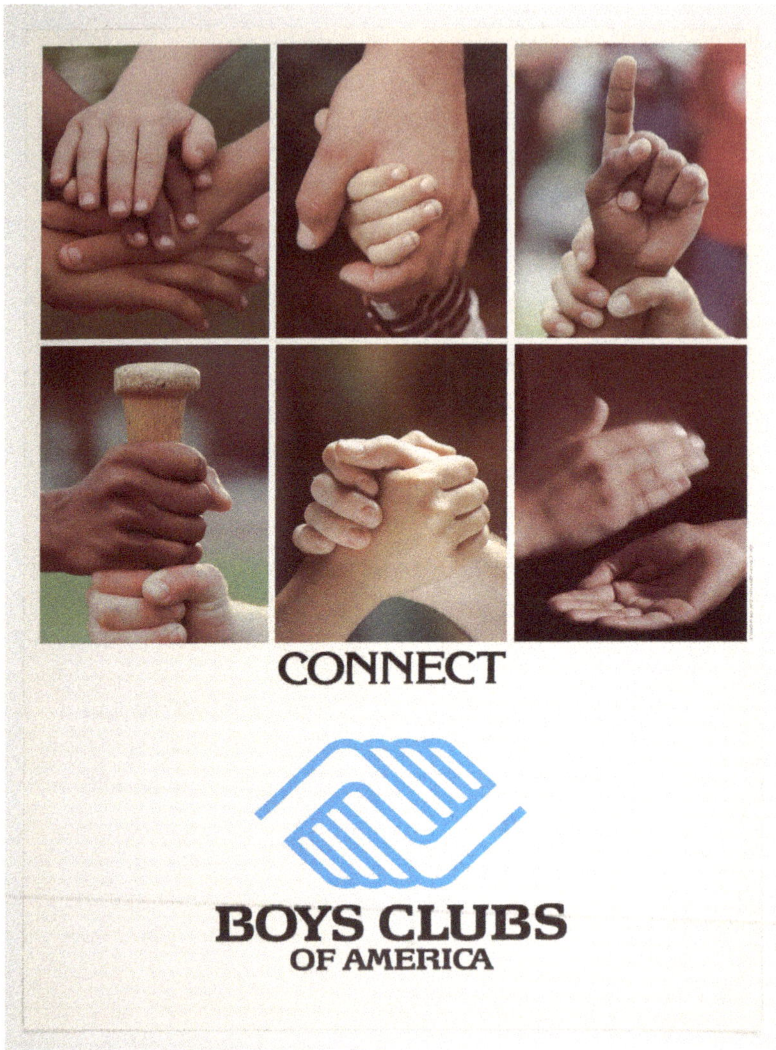

CONNECT

BOYS CLUBS
OF AMERICA

46  Bass and Kirkham, 338.

47  Michael Appert, *In Harm's Way Theatrical Movie Trailer* (produced by Otto Preminger, 1965), *YouTube* video, 4:57, June 4, 2011, https://www.youtube.com/watch?v=Nnaf9Nneb7A.

48  This image was not able to be reproduced for this book. However, it can be found online at https://filmartgallery.com/products/sba-in-harms-way.

49  Moholy-Nagy, 12.

Bass said that it "[visualizes] the primary commitment of the Boys Clubs of America: connection."[46] The abstraction of the hands allows the viewer to overlay their own experience—not necessarily with the organization, but with the organization's mission. As children, we all need connection and support from our peers and from adults. While the photographs on the poster literalize those connections, Bass's abstract hands encourage us to make them ourselves.

This emphasis on abstract design elements within a spatial field is perhaps even more dynamic in Bass's work on film publicity. Preminger's *In Harm's Way* (1965) is a film about the Pacific Theatre in World War II following the attack on Pearl Harbor. As Preminger himself describes it in a lengthy trailer for the film, it is a movie about "the will to survive" against difficult odds on the soldiers' march toward victory.[47] The film depicts the psychological struggles of dealing with tragedy and the strain of war on individuals and their relationships. Bass's poster for the film boils these themes down to a single image of an arm and a hand pointing firmly forward.[48] In the Bauhaus tradition, designers aim to integrate thought and emotion. As Moholy-Nagy notes, art should help the viewer understand "feeling and thinking in relationship and not as a series of isolated phenomena." This is what he calls "vision in motion."[49] It is, as discussed previously, about the construction of spatial relationships. However, it is more than simply the position of elements in space as described earlier. These relationships are also present in the connection between the elements and the empty, negative space. In the poster for *In Harm's Way*, Bass very much adopts this perspective. Moholy-Nagy claims that when all space is filled, art becomes static. But the relationships become stronger and

50 Horak, 64.

51 Kepes, 51.

the art more dynamic when the positive and negative spaces of the piece are placed against one another. The lack of other visual cues in the image gives an impression not just of a finger pointing, but of an arm thrusting forward. A key element of Bass's designs is "the creation of dynamic rhythms within the field of vision." Every piece of a design contributes to "a directional sense of movement through the act of reading" the image.[50]

When considering Preminger's description of his characters' "will to survive" and their psychological trauma, the arm suggests that the viewer must press on, willing themselves into an unknown future. Importantly, that future is unknown precisely because of Bass's use of the entirety of the width of the image, something that places meaning even more into flux than the use of negative space.

The use of distinct boundaries in a design traditionally creates an area that appears more stable and formed than one without such boundaries.[51] However, in this poster, the viewer is directed beyond the frame, beyond the scope of the visible (known) world. While the poster presents a boundary around the black rectangle, the arm and, notably, the pointing finger both break that boundary, blending into the margins, destabilizing the design and inserting a level of apprehension into the viewer. Much like the characters in the film, viewers are compelled to move forward, but they can only move toward uncertainty.

The thrust toward uncertainty in Bass's poster for *In Harm's Way* is accomplished by eliminating the border and destabilizing the image. We see the opposite effect in his work

52 Moholy-Nagy, 12.

53 Kepes, 52.

54 Moholy-Nagy, 28.

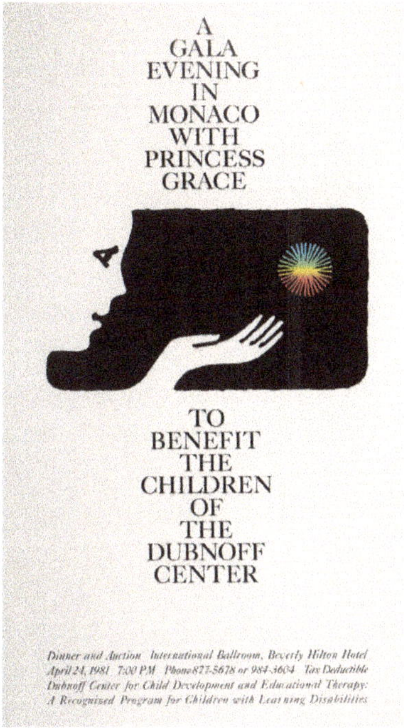

**Figure 11.**

Poster for the Princess Grace Fund (1981).
Saul Bass Collection, Cary Graphic Arts
Collection at the Wallace Library, Rochester
Institute of Technology.

for the Princess Grace Fund (see Figure 11). If vision in motion is, as Moholy-Nagy describes it, "a synonym for simultaneity and space-time," then a piece of art captures a particular moment of the integration of thought and emotion.[52] And the sense of movement brought about by the spatial relationships of the image's elements suggests ongoing change. As Kepes argues, images must also be understood "in the time dimension."[53] In this design, the uncertainty lies prior to the space-time of the image as the viewer's eyes move across from the child to the sunburst. The boundary on the left—behind the child, who is moving forward—is nonexistent. But the child appears to be moving into a defined, stable space occupied by the sunburst. At the time of the poster's design (1981), the fund's recipient had recently established residential group homes for struggling children. Bass is able to capture the sense of hope that comes with the stability of a supportive environment. The stability, represented by the enclosed right side of the image, stands as a contrast to the uncertainty being left behind.

Such uncertainty acts as only a small piece of art's humanity. One function of art is to balance social, intellectual, and emotional existence by synthesizing attitudes, fears, and hopes. As Moholy-Nagy says, "Art sensitizes man to the best that is . . . in him."[54] This is something that many say Bass

55. John Frankenheimer, speaking at the Saul Bass Memorial at the Academy of Motion Picture Arts & Sciences in Los Angeles, 1996. Saul Bass Collection, Cary Graphic Arts Collection at the Wallace Library, Rochester Institute of Technology.

56 Kepes, 221.

57 Moholy-Nagy, 25.

58 Julian Binod, speaking at the Saul Bass Celebration in New York City, May 23, 1996. Saul Bass Collection, Cary Graphic Arts Collection at the Wallace Library, Rochester Institute of Technology.

59 Horak, 46.

60 Henry Wolf, speaking at the Saul Bass Celebration in New York City, May 23, 1996. Saul Bass Collection, Cary Graphic Arts Collection at the Wallace Library, Rochester Institute of Technology.

was able to do with his designs, such as when director John Frankenheimer said at Bass's memorial at the Motion Picture Academy, Bass "was so pure and so truthful . . . he knew what truth really was."[55]

## Social Responsibility

Bass's understanding of truth motivated him throughout his life and his career as a designer. He regularly produced work in support of social and environmental causes. Bass's sense of social responsibility made Bauhaus design a perfect fit for his work. Because of the ubiquity of advertising images, Kepes viewed them as serving a dual purpose, one of which is to "disseminate socially useful messages."[56] The second role of images is to help "re-educate" the viewer into a more fully integrated life, leading to what Moholy-Nagy described as "the preservation and refinement of the biological nature of the individual within a harmonious social existence."[57] In other words, design was not merely the creation of visually pleasing pieces of advertising. Instead, it was an opportunity to affect change within both the individual and society—to raise one's awareness of their being in order to create a more unified whole. As Julian Binod noted at Bass's memorial, "His images surround us."[58] While he may have meant this literally, given the prominence of Bass's work, it is also a metaphorical way to think about Bass's designs. From a Bauhaus perspective, art should integrate all of the varied pieces of human experience and interaction.[59] And Bass, as described by graphic designer Henry Wolf, attempted to "[create] in us an image that he wanted us to have."[60] In other words, Bass's work provided a model for human experience and understanding.

61 Bass and Kirkham, 328.

In the Bass worldview, we are always reaching, striving for more perfect selves and a better society. As noted earlier, this characteristic in his work often takes the form of hands. There is, of course, the iconic hand from *The Man with the Golden Arm* and the thrusting, pointing hand on the poster for *In Harm's Way*, but hands are even more prominent in his non-film work. For example, in the Princess Grace Fund poster, the child reaches toward stability and hope. The clasping hands in the logo for the Boys and Girls Clubs of America, discussed previously, show hands as a way of providing support. In Bass's world, we reach for one another, pulling one another to safety, and we don't let go. This is also evident in Bass's logo for United Way (see Figure 12). In the logo, a stylized human figure stands supported by a hand and enclosed by a rainbowlike design, which Bass referred to as a "rainbow of hope."[61] Like the child's hand in the Princess Grace Fund poster—but unlike the hand in *The Man with the*

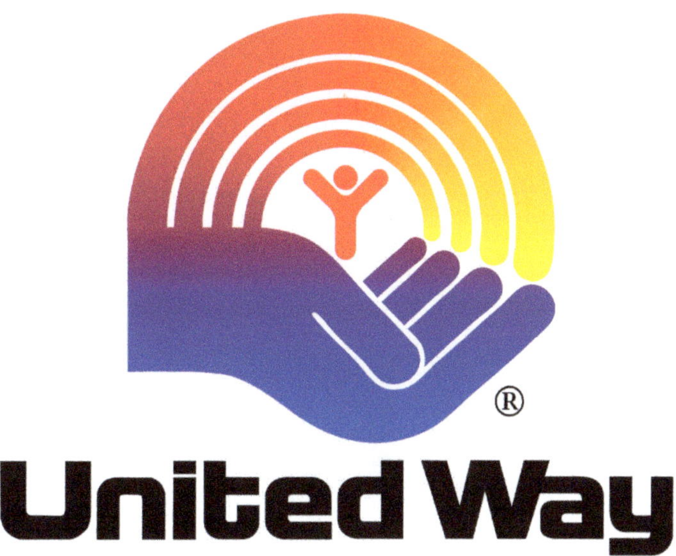


**Figure 12.**

United Way logo (1972).

*Golden Arm*—the hand is open rather than grasping. The open hand suggests a gentle catching movement, such as what one may do when attempting to catch a delicate object that needs to be treated with care. There was some concern at the organization that it was difficult to tell if the hand was giving or receiving, yet Bass viewed this as a strength of the design. Indeed, as the rainbow emerges from the hand, the viewer sees the logo as giving hope to the charity's recipients as well as receiving them into a positive, safe space. Additionally, considering the concept of boundaries as providing stability, the hand in this case provides not only support and safety for those in need, but also, through its connection to the rainbow, stability.

The twin themes of reaching and safety are also present in two of Bass's posters produced thirty years apart and promoting two very different programs. In a poster for the 1989 International Winter Games of the Special Olympics (see Figure 13), Bass depicts a human form with wings rising into the sky and reaching for a star. While the viewer may at first be drawn to the wings, the motion of the figure places the image's emphasis on the extended hands and the object of their desire. Here, the reaching hands are aspirational. As if to reinforce this, Bass places the event's motto in the field of stars at the top of the image. Visually, the words parallel the movement of the figure and, as representative of stars, connect the motto's ideals of honor and bravery to the rising star just within the figure's reach.

In the second poster, Bass provides an image of hands that are equally as aspirational, though from a different direction. The National Committee for a Sane Nuclear Policy (SANE, now known as Peace Action), an organization dedicated to ending nuclear proliferation and steering American opinion away from war, was widely supported in Hollywood and ran a series of newspaper advertisements signed by prominent leaders. In 1959, Bass created a symbol for the Hollywood branch of SANE and produced "For a Sane Nuclear Policy" (see Figure 14). Here, the hands are still reaching, but they

**Figure 13.**

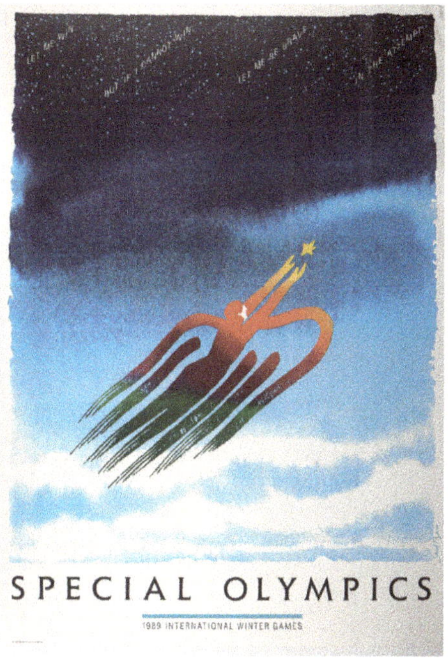


Special Olympics Poster (1989). Saul Bass Collection, Cary Graphic Arts Collection at the Wallace Library, Rochester Institute of Technology.

*The Special Olympics logo and the name "Special Olympics" is reproduced with the kind permission of Special Olympics, Inc., Washington, DC [www.specialolympics.org].*

**Figure 14.**

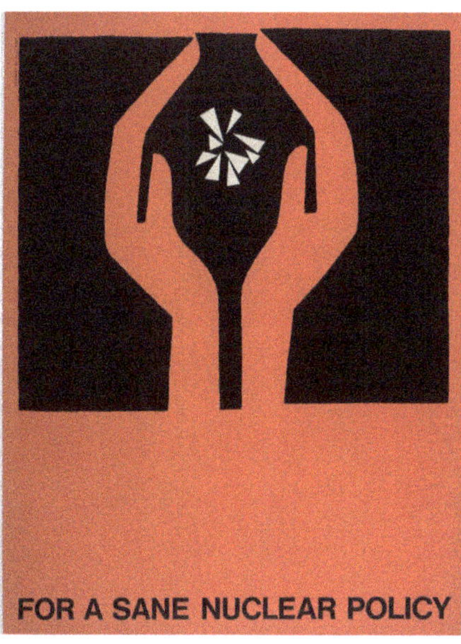


For a Sane Nuclear Policy Poster (1959). Saul Bass Collection, Cary Graphic Arts Collection at the Wallace Library, Rochester Institute of Technology.

are also protecting. The hands enclose the splintered star of nuclear weapons, both containing and shielding it. The image suggests that if the power of nuclear weapons is to be held by human hands, they should also be humane hands. As the caption suggests, this is not necessarily a call for the end of nuclear weapons, but for their responsible handling. In this way, the image is just as hopeful as the figure on the Special Olympics poster. Together, they provide great insight into Bass's understanding of the world.

**Figure 15.**

Poster for *Why Man Creates* (1968). Saul Bass Collection, Cary Graphic Arts Collection at the Wallace Library, Rochester Institute of Technology.

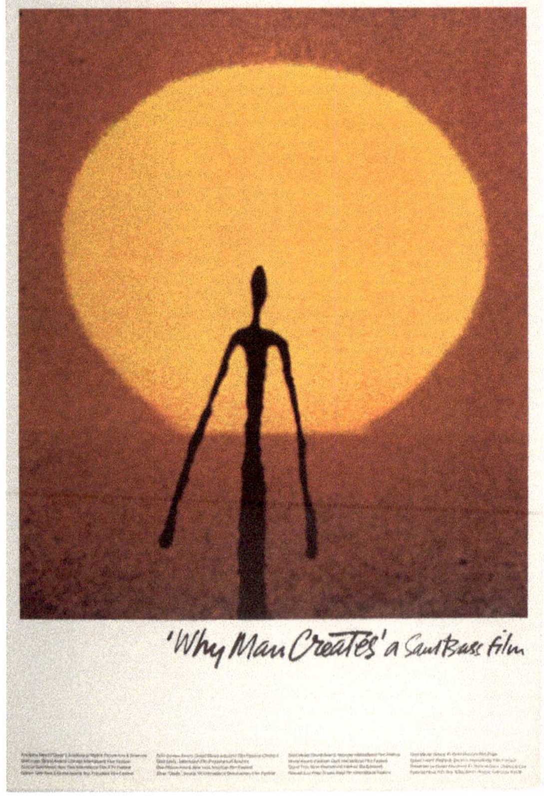

62 Horak, 68.

63 Bass and Kirkham, 241.

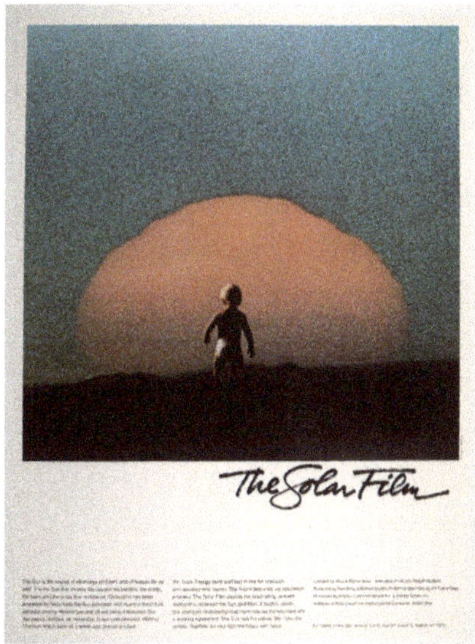

**Figure 16.**

Poster for *The Solar Film* (1980). Saul Bass Collection, Cary Graphic Arts Collection at the Wallace Library, Rochester Institute of Technology.

In addition to the hands in these works, there are hints of another common motif in Bass's work: the sun or star. Even in the United Way logo, the colors—with the brightest yellow and orange on the right/east side of the image—suggest a rising sun. One of the key elements of Bauhaus design, as well as an important piece of Bass's style, is the use of simple shapes such as lines, squares, and circles. The circle lies at the heart of Bass's two primary philosophical influences. In Gestalt psychology, the circle is central to human biology and survival, as it recalls the shape of a predator's eye. In Bauhaus design, "the circle represents continuous or infinite movement" and is "a self-enclosed form," communicating a sense of independence to the viewer.[62] This is combined with the imagery of the sun and its implications for giving life and representing hope. The sun figures prominently in Bass's posters for his own films. In his Oscar-winning short documentary, *Why Man Creates* (1968), Bass presents a distorted image of a person silhouetted against the sun (see Figure 15). In *The Solar Film* (1980), the poster depicts a toddler walking toward the sun (see Figure 16). These documentaries were typical of Bass's preference for projects funded by sponsors with an interest in advocacy or image building. The first, a film about humanity's endless creativity, was sponsored by Kaiser Aluminum and Chemical Company, whose CEO at the time "believed strongly that creativity and imagination were the lifeblood of change and that big business should show itself to be socially responsible."[63] The second film, about the promise of solar energy, was produced by Robert Redford through his association with the environmental group Consumer Action Now and largely financed by Warner Communications, for whom Bass had recently completed a logo design.

When viewed independently, the two posters provide some insight into Bass's thoughts concerning the ideas presented in their respective films. Perhaps most striking about the image for *Why Man Creates* is the shape of the human silhouette. It is elongated and made to appear thin, reminiscent of figures associated with ancient or tribal drawings. Such an image indicates that the roots of humanity's creativity are buried deep within us as a species and, critically, the use of the sun presents the viewer with a constant with which we can link modern creativity with our ancient selves. But it also links creativity with the life, hope, and independence associated with the sun and the circle. The stretching of the figure suggests that it is both rising and moving toward the sun in a direction up and away from the viewer. The sun is setting, and the figure seems to wish to follow it. In other words, humans create, and have always created, as a means of growth and as a journey central to our humanity. People create in order to continue their rise as a species. In some ways, Bass returns to this concept in his poster for *The Solar Film*. This time, however, the sun is rising, and the figure is clearly a young child. The sun here is no longer a symbol of humanity's aspirations, but rather a representation of a bright future to come. As with the hope that is inherent in images of the sun, similar ideals are typically associated with images of youth and their presumably bright futures.

When these images are taken together, they present a single narrative. In the first, the sun is setting as the figure strives for achievement. Creativity is at the heart of that potential and is necessary for the continued rise of humanity. If humanity stretches far enough, if its creativity is harnessed for the good of the species, then as the sun rises, as in the second, humanity can move forward with a promise for a better future. Indeed, Bass's association with the rising sun as a symbol of hope for the future is made explicit in his poster for the YWCA, in which women join hands to welcome the rising sun, accompanied by the caption, "Celebrate a New Beginning" (see Figure 17).

**Figure 17.**

YWCA Poster (1988). Saul Bass Collection, Cary Graphic Arts Collection at the Wallace Library, Rochester Institute of Technology.

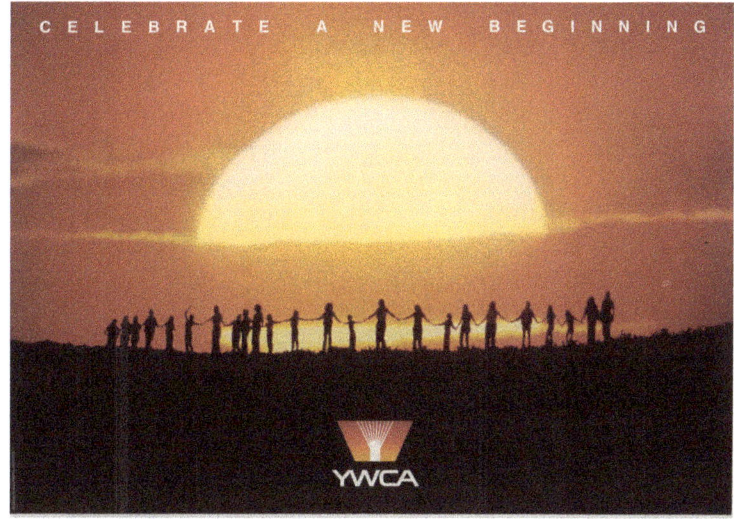


## Personal Work

The need for creative thinking regarding our energy demands is central to the message of *The Solar Film*, and the concept of hope for a better future is an essential piece of some of Bass's most personal work. The SANE logo and poster project, described previously, was an early example of the type of work that Bass referred to as his "personal handwriting," which would go on to include works such as *Why Man Creates* and *The Solar Film* (both of which, incidentally,

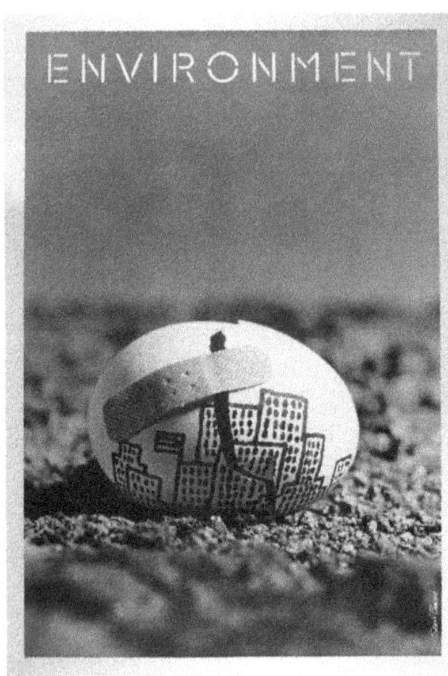



**Figure 18.**

*Environment* (1971). Saul Bass Collection, Cary Graphic Arts Collection at the Wallace Library, Rochester Institute of Technology.

feature their titles written in Bass's handwriting on the posters). They were projects that he completed, often pro bono, for clients (including the corporate sponsors of his short films) who would let him explore ideas without interference. These were usually for causes or organizations with which Bass's sympathies aligned.[64] This includes work that he did for Human Rights Watch, various film festivals, and in support of environmental causes. In a project for *Environment* magazine, Bass continued to play with the concept of protection evident in the SANE design, although the hands are absent here (see Figure 18). The environment is fragile, represented as an eggshell. And, perhaps more important, it is already damaged. The bandage suggests that it is our responsibility to attempt to repair that damage and protect it from further harm. Just as we are caretakers for one another in Bass's work in other areas, we must also be caretakers of the environment. In an interesting reversal of the concept of "Mother Earth," Bass presents people as Earth's Mother, placing the proverbial bandage on the injury. Just as there is a lack of condemnation in the SANE design, there are no accusations of who or what has caused the damage. There is only a call for protection. However, while the presence of the hands on the SANE poster encourages the viewer with hope for containment, the lack of such symbols of support and protection in the *Environment* piece portrays the environment as vulnerable, and the image is one of concern. And here lies another important function of the hands: they signify a human connection, and the presence of humanity is reassuring. While we are meant to protect the fragile environment and even acknowledge that responsibility, as evidenced by the bandage, we have nonetheless left the egg on its own, vulnerable to future damage. This concern for the environment is one Bass would take up in his own film work,

65 Horak, 218.

most notably in *The Solar Film*. He would also address his own concept of humanity and its relationship to the world in his Oscar-winning film *Why Man Creates*.

*The Solar Film* is presented in three parts. The first segment describes humanity's historical relationship to the sun. The second is an animation depicting the industrial revolution, followed by the final section, which advocates for the adoption of solar power. The film begins with a sunrise over what the narrator describes as "a young, barren Earth." The film then depicts the rise of human civilization, framing it as a by-product of the sun's energy. The narrator asks the question: "How was primitive man to deal with the power that controlled his life? Power that could provide or deny?" Throughout the opening segment of the film, Bass makes use of montage, focusing on the power of images rather than words. This reflects his sensibility as a designer who was more comfortable creating images to move a viewer rather than constructing longer sequences and narratives involving distinct plots or actors.[65] Near the end of the first segment, the narrator claims that "the more he [*sic*] learned, the less he feared. And knowledge only increased his awe." Here, there is evidence of some connections to the point of view Bass had established twelve years earlier in *Why Man Creates*.

Like *The Solar Film, Why Man Creates* provides little narrative structure and is instead a collection of vignettes that convey thematic meaning. In the earlier film, Bass makes the claim that humans are driven by a desire to understand themselves, their world, and their place in it. The film begins with a segment titled "The Edifice," an animated sequence in which the progression of human knowledge is imagined as a building rising higher and higher through the centuries. The Edifice explores inventions of necessity such as the wheel and, later, the inventions of ideas. The narrator explains that ideas emerge when a person looks at one thing and sees another. The film culminates with a question about the origins of the universe, then a series of observations about creativity itself. In the film's loose narrative, human creativity grows from necessity to a deeper understanding and consideration of the human condition. In the film's opening scene, an animated caveman is frightened by a large animal he is hunting. This event provides the foundation for The Edifice. In the closing scene, we see a child running through a flock of birds as the narrator explains that people create in order to be able to look out from themselves and say, "I am unique. I am here. I am."

As in *The Solar Film*, Bass sees a progression from fear to awe of the world, if not the universe. And it is creativity that drives us forward. Ultimately, in Bass's vision, such creativity can lead to better solutions for the problems we face. In one segment of *Why Man Creates*, a man struggles to build a sculpture with a collection of foam blocks. After he accidentally puts his hand through one of the blocks, he is struck with an idea to use mannequin parts in his sculpture. He is subsequently ridiculed for his ideas. This mirrors pieces of The Edifice, in which ideas such as the Earth being round or everyone having a say in government are shut behind doors or otherwise silenced. The viewer knows, however, that such ideas would become the foundation of modern science and political philosophy, suggesting that the artist's creation will one day also be embraced by the society that had rejected it. This implies a very important element of Bass's worldview. As noted earlier, Bass views humanity's penchant

66  Walter R. Fisher, *Human Communication as Narration: Toward a Philosophy of Reason, Value, and Action* (Columbia: University of South Carolina Press, 1987), 5.

67  Hayden White, "The Value of Narrativity in the Representation of Reality," *Critical Inquiry* 7, no. 1 (1980): 5–27.

for creativity and hope as embedded deep within the species' genetic makeup. Both of these films begin at the dawn of human civilization and follow the thread of progress toward enlightenment emerging from creativity. Bass's optimism that good ideas are eventually embraced reflects his belief in the ultimate goodness of human nature.

**Telling Stories**

Much of Bass's work relies on a basic construction of narrative, even if a plot is not necessarily present. This is, in part, related to the Bauhaus concepts of motion and spatial relationships among elements within a design, as discussed earlier. But when thinking of Bass's projects as narratives, they must be considered as more than assemblages of graphic elements that might be experienced in sequence. To rhetorical theorist Walter Fisher, humans are inherently storytellers, and narratives permeate our everyday discourse. Indeed, he says the very "world as we know it is a set of stories."[66] More specifically, historian Hayden White explains that narrative is not merely a sequence of events, but rather a "chronological framework" that provides "an order of meaning" that the events would not otherwise possess.[67] This is especially evident in Bass's documentaries. Both of his major documentary films are constructed as montages. They move more or less chronologically but ultimately derive their meanings from the *relationships* established in their order. For instance, in *Why Man Creates*, the sequence involving the sculptor and his mannequin parts gleans its meaning from its position in the film *after* The Edifice, which depicts the initial rejection of brilliant ideas. While chronologically it occurs later than the earlier segment, it is in no way related to the events of The Edifice. Instead, it gains its meaning due to the

68 Bass and Kirkham, 250.

69 Horak, 221.

70 Wayne C. Booth, *The Rhetoric of Fiction,* 2nd ed. (Chicago: University of Chicago Press, 1983), xiii.

relationship established between the segments. It holds little meaning on its own, but when placed in sequence it becomes a powerful illustration of a concept explored earlier in the film. A similar technique is at work in *The Solar Film*. As Bass and Kirkham describe the documentary, "Each section makes its point effectively, but viewers also absorb a wider message about the power of the sun."[68]

In the press release for *The Solar Film*, Bass said that he and his wife, Elaine, who codirected the film—receiving her first joint directorial credit for any project on which they had collaborated—had hoped to "encourage people to think more and more about the subject" of solar energy.[69] To this end, the film concludes with the image that would become the poster: the toddler walking toward the rising sun. On-screen text reads: "The sun gave us a world, it can give us a future." In each of these independent film projects, his most prominent works as a filmmaker, he tells the same story. If Bass was, as Henry Wolf said, creating a picture of the world that he wanted the viewer to have as their own, then he certainly made it a point to share his love for humanity and his hope for the future. His ability to do so is rooted in his knack for creating narratives within his work. As rhetorician Wayne Booth has argued about the use of narrative, an author—or, in this case, a designer—is able to "impose [their] world upon" the audience.[70] From this perspective on narrative, the audience is persuaded to accept, at least for a time, a certain vision of how the world is or should be.

71 Seymour Chatman, *Coming to Terms:
The Rhetoric of Narrative in Fiction and Film*
(Ithaca, NY: Cornell University Press).

72 Bass and Kirkham, 250.

This is particularly important when considering *The Solar Film*. If Bass's intention was to encourage people to seriously consider the potential of solar energy through the construction of a specific vision of the world, then he is serving what Seymour Chatman has called a constitutive function of narrative.[71] For Chatman, narratives are inherently ideological and serve either an instrumental or a constitutive function. In their constitutive form, they attempt to affect how the audience understands its world and offer encouragement for the literal transformation of that world. It was important for Saul and Elaine Bass to make sure their message was embedded within the images and not stated too explicitly. In one interview, Saul noted that they "had to constantly guard against didacticism" and feared that certain segments became too "preachy, pretentious, [or] politically correct."[72] Here, Bass is explicitly rejecting what Chatman refers to as the instrumental function of narrative. Chatman refers to didactic narratives as those that do not merely reflect a particular worldview, but rather attempt to make a clear and obvious point. When doing so, such narratives usually respond to a specific situation. The sequence Bass referred to in his interview includes characters specifically demanding that the government "do something" about solar energy. Bass consciously avoids this approach throughout the rest of the film, opting instead to argue for a broader social transformation.

Narrative is a consistent presence in Bass's work, even in cases where he is not necessarily making an obvious argument. For instance, his corporate work makes use of narrative as a way to define an experience. As discussed earlier, the Bauhaus school of design was centered upon the idea of motion and

73 Lee Roy Beach, "Decision making: Linking narratives and action," *Narrative Inquiry* 19, no. 2 (2009): 393–414.

74 Beach, 394.

75 Beach, 399.

change over time. From this perspective, art integrates thought and emotion through the creation of a visual experience. A large component of Bauhaus design theory, as laid out by Kepes, is Gestalt psychology, and a major element of the Gestalt perspective is a focus on the whole of an object rather than its constituent parts. And thinking about how the different elements of a design fit together into a coherent whole, along with the ideas of movement, results in a way by which to consider the role of narrative in design and in the creation of a visual experience.

A more modern psychological perspective takes the concept of narrative one step further, arguing that a narrative thought process can create concrete action.[73] Psychologist Lee Roy Beach describes narratives as "a rich mixture of memories and [images] laced together by emotions."[74] This psychological perspective's focus on memories and images leads to the belief that words only serve to "impoverish" the narrative, a concept not unlike Kepes's own understanding of design; for example, his book *The Language of Vision* is missing any detailed discussion of typography. In narrative psychology, stories suggest a potential future, which results in the creation of a plan, defined as "a sequence of potential actions designed to influence crucial junctures" in order to create a "desirable future."[75] This sequence is established through "tactics," what one might think of as individual plot points. Decision-making starts with an evaluation of the future's desirability, which is evaluated based on one's memory of previous narratives. Bass demonstrates this concept in his design plan for Exxon service stations, which would eventually come to define the look of the modern gas station.

76  Bass and Kirkham, 355.

77  The Bell Systems pitch film is freely available at https://www.youtube.com/watch?v=xKu2deoyCJI.

## The Cone of Vision

Exxon approached Bass and Yager in 1977 to design a consistent branding plan that they could apply in part to older service stations and to fully implement in new stations. Bass was able to convince them that they needed a complete redesign, not simply an update. He noted that gas-station design is typically done by architects; graphic designers are brought in later. He argued that "this was putting the cart before the horse. A service station is really a retail store and should be conceived as such . . . [let us] design it and then we'll bring the architects in to make sure it doesn't fall down."[76] The background and design plan were presented to the company in 1981 in the form of a corporate film intended for internal use only. The film itself is quite similar to Bass's documentary film style first established in *Why Man Creates*. While the Exxon film is not available publicly, its format is similar to that used for Bass's Bell Systems pitch in 1969.[77] It begins with a montage of images showing rising gas prices, signs referring to gas shortages, and a list of new cultural conditions. It suggests that "increased clutter leads to the visual erosion of the station." From there, it describes the design firm's worldwide survey of existing stations (personnel visited twenty-five cities in fourteen countries) and its conclusion that the new stations should focus on retail services with a flexible and modular design, which is laid out in the second half of the film. While the design presentation itself is fairly standard, Bass's redesign of the Exxon system, perhaps more than any of his other designs, would transform the American visual landscape.

78  *Exxon Corporate Film*, DVD, produced by
    Bass and Yager (1981). Saul Bass Collection,
    Cary Graphic Arts Collection at the Wallace
    Library, Rochester Institute of Technology.

Prior to the development of the new Exxon stations, service stations were each unique in many ways. While most had canopies covering the gas pumps and all had signage, the design was largely left to station owners and built to fit within their environment. There was little consistency between stations and even less coherence within individual stations. Bass's design for Exxon did not necessarily insist that all stations be identical, but rather that they reflect and serve as a clear part of a larger system. This system reflected an emphasis on adaptability across time and geographic regions as well as a shift away from industrial design and toward retail design. These concepts led to a number of architectural elements that would become standard in new stations—not only for Exxon, but for virtually all service-station brands. The film states that Exxon's viewpoint was that "the service station is a tangible representation of the Corporation to much of the public."[78] In other words, the service stations themselves were viewed much like a corporate logo, and Bass approached the project in a similar manner, taking not merely the movement of the customer's eyes to understand the narrative, but also the movement of their entire body.
The film describes the concept of a "cone of vision" that follows a customer as they move toward and through the service station. The content and design of signage and structures were connected directly to anticipated customer movement. In Beach's terms, Bass considered the "sequence of potential actions" and designed accordingly. In this way, narrative and design came together in order to create a positive experience for the customer, which, of course, would create positive results for Exxon.

Establishing the cone of vision was essential to Bass's design. He took into account what a customer would experience from the street, into the parking lot, under the canopy, and into the retail space. To accomplish this, the firm built a full-size model of their design on a ranch in California. As a customer approaches along the street, the canopy itself serves as a sign, as opposed to a separate sign or one mounted on the top of the canopy. As they move into the parking lot, the cone of vision shifts. Since the canopy is no longer visible, Bass added what he called "spreaders" between the columns to serve as a brand reminder during the pumping process. According to the film, this would "[fix] the location in the mind's eye." Additionally, the columns were expanded in order to give a sense of "visible quality and strength." Another innovation in the design was to insert lighting systems inside the spreaders in order to give the customer more of a retail experience, even in the areas outside of the retail store.

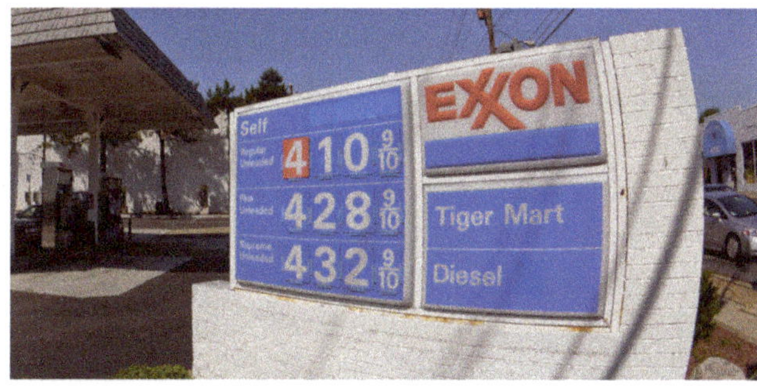


**Figure 19.**

Exxon service station sign.
Rob Crandall / Alamy Stock Photo.

Another major aspect of Bass's Exxon design that would become an industry standard was the modular signage. Here, the focus was on interchangeability. Since different geographic regions and different stations would have different needs, Bass considered interchangeable signage as a solution that would maintain the system's consistency (see Figure 19). Placing the logo at the top with rectangles designated for each aspect of the station's services allowed the design to remain consistent across stations. The idea of modularity also figured into the

79 *BP Reimage Project: A New Beginning,* DVD, produced by Bass and Yager (1989). Saul Bass Collection, Cary Graphic Arts Collection at the Wallace Library, Rochester Institute of Technology.

**Figure 20.**

Esso (Exxon) service station. Note the two individual "boxes" in the building's design. Imago / Alamy Stock Photo.

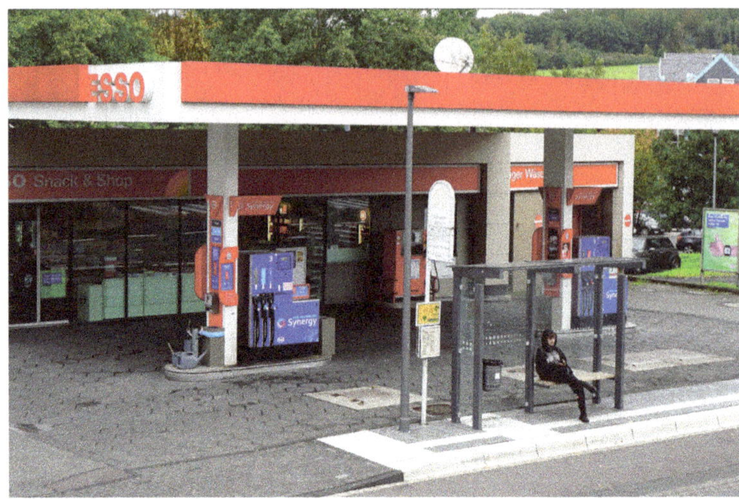


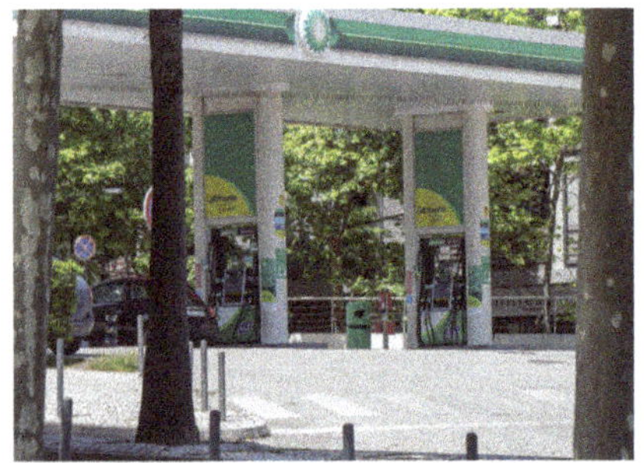

**Figure 21.**

BP Service Station.
Wirestock, Inc. / Alamy Stock Photo.

buildings themselves. Each section of the retail space was considered a box, making the services modular as well. In this way, a station could be designed, built, or altered in a way that best met its individual needs (see Figure 20).

Bass would revisit this approach to gas-station design in a similar project completed for BP in 1989.[79] Though the presentation film for the latter project is a more conventional corporate film, without the stylized montages of its Exxon counterpart, the thought process and, ultimately, the design are very similar. The primary difference between them is another design innovation that has become commonplace. Rather than using spreaders between columns, the design features a branding pillar above each pump (see Figure 21).

In these gas-station designs, which included those for affiliated brands such as Esso, Mobil (after its merger with Exxon in the 1990s), Sohio, and Gulf, Bass established himself as not only

   GRAPHIC DESIGN ARCHIVES CHAPBOOK SERIES

80  Wolf von Eckardt, "Creating Good-Looking Objects That Work," *Time* 119, no. 1 (1982): 82.

81  Mark Deuze, Media Life (Boston: Polity Press, 2012).

a filmmaker and an artist, but an industrial and architectural designer as well. The Exxon design was named in 1981 to *Time* magazine's ten best "good-looking objects that work," describing it as a "quietly assertive unit that should help calm America's roadside clutter."[80] Although one could argue that roadside clutter has actually increased during the intervening years, one would be hard pressed to find another design—or designer—that has had as large of an impact on American visual culture.

Again, modern web design highlights evidence of Bass's lasting influence, even in the concept of the Cone of Vision. Media theorist Mark Deuze argues that people live within media—it has become our architecture and, in many cases, our retail space. And, importantly, people are no more aware of the structure of those spaces than fish are of the water in which they live.[81] The goal of modern web designers is to create an experience in which the user moves seamlessly from one page or content area to another. We can see this in the way we scroll through a website. On one hand, we have the endless scroll of a social media site. But on the other hand, scrolling is our primary physical interaction with a website, so providing clear visual feedback to the scrolling is important. Just as Bass's customers moved through the different and clearly demarcated sections of the Exxon design, today's web users often see changes to colors, animations, or altered layouts. And, in the spirit of Bass's activism and sense of responsibility, web design is also likely to follow a larger cultural trend of social and environmental awareness. As designer Tristan Le Breton has noted, more brands are attempting to connect to users on issues that are important to them, and the near future of user-interface design is likely to include imagery that

82 99designs Team, "9 stunning web design trends
for 2021," https://99designs.com/blog/trends/web-
design-trends/.

83 Steven Spielberg, in a letter read by Lou Dorfsman
at the Saul Bass Celebration in New York City,
May 23, 1996. Saul Bass Collection, Cary Graphic
Arts Collection at the Wallace Library, Rochester
Institute of Technology.

84 Robert Thomas, Jr., "Saul Bass, 75, Designer,
Dies; Made Art Out of Movie Titles," *New York
Times*, April 27, 1996, 30.

85 Ivan Chermayeff, speaking at the Tribute to Saul
Bass at the International Design Conference in
Aspen, June 6, 1996. Saul Bass Collection, Cary
Graphic Arts Collection at the Wallace Library,
Rochester Institute of Technology.

86 David Brown, in a letter read by Herb Yager
at the Saul Bass Memorial at the Motion
Picture Academy in Los Angeles, 1996. Saul
Bass Collection, Cary Graphic Arts Collection
at the Wallace Library, Rochester Institute of
Technology.

resonates with "social [and] environmental issues."[82]
While scrolling effects and social and environmental
awareness are not necessarily design trends directly related
to Bass's work, they are nonetheless reflective of ideas that
guided him and that he found important in the creation of
effective, meaningful art.

### Enduring Visibility

Saul Bass passed away on April 25, 1996, of non-Hodgkin's
lymphoma. There were at least three public memorials for him
and his work. A letter from Steven Spielberg was read at the
first of them, held in New York City. Spielberg described Bass,
saying, "His body of work qualifies him as one of the best
filmmakers of this or any other time."[83] Bass was, of course,
best known for his work in the film industry, especially
for his revolution of the film title sequence. *The New York
Times* described him "as the man who invented the opening
credit sequence as a free-standing movie-before-a-movie and
elevated it into an art."[84] He has forty-two movie credits
to his name, including those for his work with Preminger,
Scorsese, and Alfred Hitchcock. But as important as his film
work is, Bass's influence extends far beyond that industry.
Society continues to experience his work in corporate logos
and architectural design through its daily encounters with
them. His images do indeed surround us. Additionally,
Bass's art has had a tremendous effect on the world of
design. As Ivan Chermayeff said at the Saul Bass tribute at
the International Design Conference in Aspen, Bass's work
"was and is and always will be a beacon for thousands of
designers."[85] David Brown, former president of Art Center
College of Design, wrote that "what Saul did and who he was
defined an entire profession."[86] Bass did indeed define what

87  Rupal Parekh, "A Few of Our Favorite Saul Bass Logos," *Advertising Age*, May 8, 2013, https://adage.com.

88  Ralph Kaplan, speaking at the Tribute to Saul Bass at the International Design Conference in Aspen, June 6, 1996. Saul Bass Collection, Cary Graphic Arts Collection at the Wallace Library, Rochester Institute of Technology.

it means to be a graphic designer. He created dozens of logos for some of the most recognizable brands in America, many of which are still in use in some form today. He pioneered the idea that a logo could be iconic not just of a brand, but of that brand's values. He was so effective at doing this that the average life span of a Saul Bass logo is more than thirty-four years.[87] He also changed the experience of watching a movie—perfecting the art of distilling a film's tone, story, and meaning in a sequence of animated credits. We see evidence of his lasting influence in designs such as the poster for *Catch Me If You Can* (directed by Steven Spielberg, 2002), the cover of The White Stripes' single "The Hardest Button to Button" (2003), and the credit sequence of AMC's *Mad Men* (2007). Those who imitate him, along with examples of work influenced by and reflective of his art, are innumerable and inescapable.

After devising a new method for putting tissues into a box, Kleenex hired Bass to convince consumers that they could fit more tissues into the same-sized package, telling him to "make the truth believable."[88] This skill was at the heart of Bass's designs. His ability to boil the meaning of an entire film into a three-minute animated credit sequence or to capture the values of an organization in a single iconic image demonstrates an innate grasping of artistic and narrative Truth. Saul Bass shared that truth with us all and made us want to see it for ourselves. Gordon Davidson once said that for Bass, "the substance is more important than the style." But for Saul Bass, the two were inseparable: the style *was* the substance. Bass's style was inarguably innovative in the way he made functional design beautiful. In his hands, corporate values became art and art became accessible. And, as all great art does, Bass's designs moved and continue to move us. His work tells the story of the latter half of the twentieth century as we struggled through social change and embraced the promise of the future. But it also tells the story of our everyday individual lives. Whether we know it or not, we have all been touched by the work of Saul Bass. And that, in the end, is the point. Bass's style is an invitation to the viewer to explore and construct meaning along with the artist. Bass's substance is the experience that emerges from that exploration and the way the process of thinking is made visible.

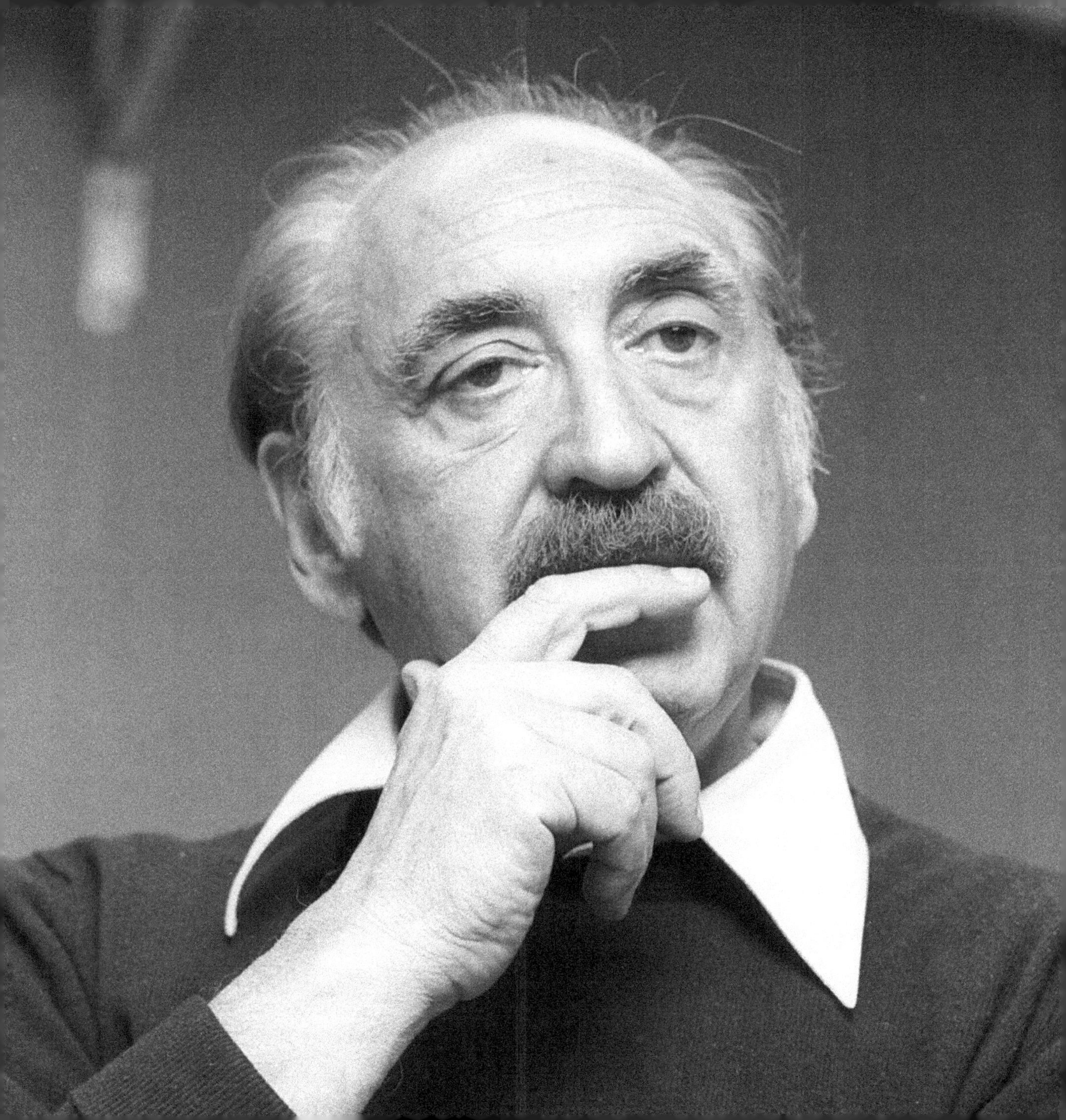

# BIBLIOGRAPHY

Appert, Michael. *In Harm's Way Theatrical Movie Trailer. YouTube* video, 4:57. June 4, 2011. Produced by Otto Preminger, 1965. https://www.youtube.com/watch?v=Nnaf9Nneb7A.

AT&T Tech Channel. *AT&T Archives: Saul Bass Pitch Video for Bell System Logo Redesign. YouTube* video, 26:59. November 30, 2011. AT&T, 1969. https://www.youtube.com/watch?v=xKu2deoyCJI.

Borgratti, Prince. *Reaching Out in New Directions. YouTube* video, 1:00. March 26, 2013. AT&T, 1984. https://www.youtube.com/watch?v=hNBwowoe2WA.

Bass, Jennifer, and Pat Kirkham. *Saul Bass: A Life in Film & Design.* London: Laurence King Publishing, 2011.

Beach, Lee Roy. "Decision making: Linking narratives and action." *Narrative Inquiry* 19, no. 2 (2009): 393–414.

Booth, Wayne C. *The Rhetoric of Fiction*, 2nd ed. Chicago: University of Chicago Press, 1983.

BP. *BP Reimage Project: A New Beginning.* Hollywood, CA: Bass and Yager, 1989. DVD held in the Saul Bass Collection, Cary Graphic Arts Collection at the Wallace Library, Rochester Institute of Technology.

Chatman, Seymour. *Coming to Terms: The Rhetoric of Narrative in Fiction and Film.* Ithaca, NY: Cornell University Press, 1990.

Dubnoff Center. "About the Dubnoff Center for Child Development." Dubnoff Center website. http://www.dubnoffcenter.org. Accessed May 22, 2019.

Exxon-Mobil. *Exxon Corporate Pitch Film.* Hollywood, CA: Bass and Yager, 1981. DVD held in the Saul Bass Collection, Cary Graphic Arts Collection at the Wallace Library, Rochester Institute of Technology.

Field, Richard S., Mel Bochner, Yale University Art Gallery, Bruce Boice, Yve-Alain Bois, James Meyer, and Rosalind E. Kraus. *Mel Bochner: Thought Made Visible 1966–1973.* New Haven, CT: Yale University Art Gallery, 1995.

Fisher, Walter R. *Human Communication as Narration: Toward a Philosophy of Reason, Value, and Action.* Columbia, SC: University of South Carolina Press, 1987.

Haskin, Pamela. "Saul, Can You Make Me a Title? Interview with Saul Bass." *Film Quarterly* 50, no. 1 (1996): 10–17.

Horak, Jan-Christopher. *Saul Bass: Anatomy of Film Design.* Lexington: University of Kentucky Press, 2014.

Kepes, Gyorgy. *Language of Vision.* Chicago: Paul Theobald, 1944.

Moholy-Nagy, Laszlo. *Vision in Motion.* Chicago: Paul Theobald, 1947.

"Saul Bass Celebration." New York City, May 23, 1996.

Saul Bass Collection, Cary Graphic Arts Collection at the Wallace Library, Rochester Institute of Technology.

Scorsese, Martin. Foreword to *Saul Bass: A Life in Film & Design*, by Jennifer Bass and Pat Kirkham, vi–vii. London: Laurence King Publishing, 2011.

Stevens, Catherine J, and Shirley McKechnie. "Thinking in Action: Thought Made Visible in Contemporary Dance." *Cognitive Processing* (2005): 243–52.

Thomas, Jr., Robert. "Saul Bass, 75, Designer, Dies; Made Art Out of Movie Titles." *New York Times*, April 27, 1996.

*Variety.* "Review: *The Man with Golden Arm*." December 31, 1955.

von Eckardt, Wolf. "Creating Good-Looking Objects That Work." *Time* 119, no. 1 (1982): 82.

White, H. "The Value of Narrativity in the Representation of Reality." *Critical Inquiry* 7, no. 1 (1980): 5–27.

I'd first like to thank Kelly Norris Martin for inviting me to contribute to this chapbook series. I have always been a fan of Bass's work and have truly enjoyed the opportunity to explore it in some depth for this project. I truly appreciate her help and patience during my sometimes painfully slow writing process. I also want to thank Alexandra Hoff for her patience during that same slow process and for guiding me through the steps of finally bringing this project to print. I also want to acknowledge Kennaria Brown for her help in talking through the aspirational and protective nature of hands that turned into an important part of my interpretation of Bass's work. Finally, there are those who provided personal support throughout. Thanks to Nic, Joe, Eddy, and Josh for keeping an eye out for vintage Exxon stations even if there were none to be found. Thanks to Verlaine McDonald for assuring me that it was "not just a chapbook." Most importantly, thanks to Susan for being there and for putting up with having to listen to me talk about Saul Bass logos and gas stations and complain when I couldn't get in touch with copyright holders. Just having you near me means the world. Finally, thanks to Benjamin. Your endless energy and creativity are an inspiration every day.

**Jacob A. Dickerson**

Jacob A. Dickerson is an associate professor of communication at Berea College in Berea, Kentucky, and teaches courses in media studies and production. He received his PhD from North Carolina State University in 2012 and has published work on the connection between place and identity, the use of popular music in the classroom, and gender in country music. His work has appeared in Rhetoric Review, Public Understanding of Science, and the Kentucky Journal of Communication.

COLOPHON

| | |
|---|---|
| Editorial | Alexandra Hoff |
| Design | Keli M. DiRisio |
| Original series design | Bruce Ian Meader |
| Production | Marnie Soom<br>Keli M. DiRisio |
| Typefaces | Sabon designed by Jan Tschichold<br>and Frutiger designed by Adrian Frutiger |

www.ingramcontent.com/pod-product-compliance
Lightning Source LLC
Chambersburg PA
CBHW040400240726
48664CB00012B/1693